AF584520

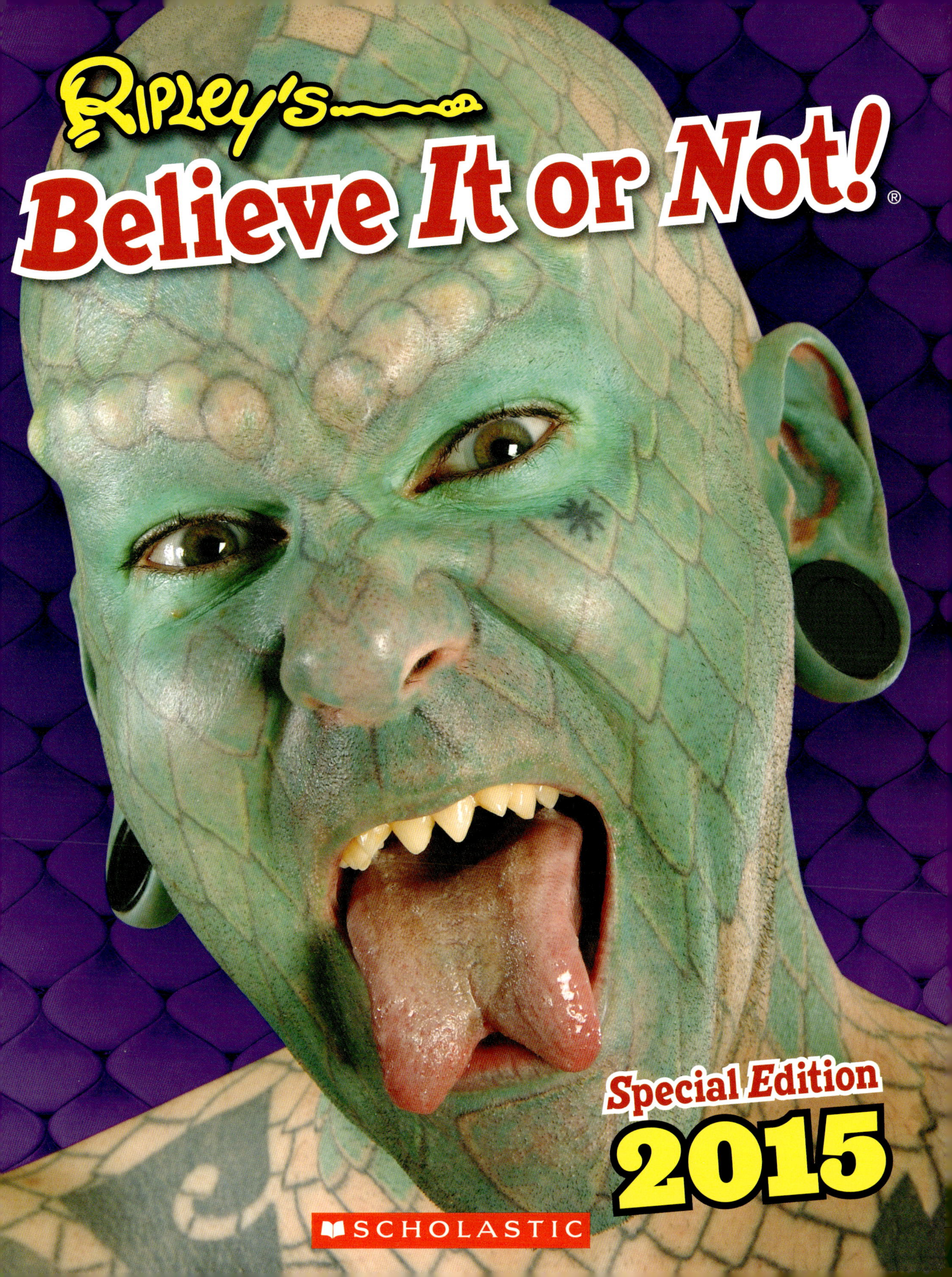
Ripley's
Believe It or Not!®
Special Edition
2015
SCHOLASTIC

page 102

Copyright © 2014 by Ripley Entertainment Inc.

All rights reserved. Ripley's, Believe It or Not!, and Ripley's Believe It or Not! are registered trademarks of Ripley Entertainment Inc. Published by Scholastic Inc. SCHOLASTIC and associated logos are trademarks and/or registered trademarks of Scholastic Inc.

No part of this publication may be reproduced in whole or in part, stored in a retrieval system, or transmitted in any form or by any means, electronic, mechanical, photocopying, recording, or otherwise, without written permission from the publisher. For information regarding permission, write to
VP Intellectual Property, Ripley Entertainment Inc., Suite 188, 7576 Kingspointe Parkway, Orlando, Florida 32819.
e-mail: publishing@ripleys.com

ISBN 978-0-545-68162-9

Developed and produced by Ripley Publishing Ltd

Publisher: Anne Marshall
Editorial Director: Becky Miles
Art Director: Sam South

Project Editor: Charlotte Howell
Senior Researcher: James Proud
Design: Rocket Design (East Anglia) Ltd
Indexer: Hilary Bird
Reprographics: Juice Creative

Cover credits: Photo © Allen Falkner; Used with permission from Erik "The Lizardman" Sprague.
10 9 8 7 6 5 4 3 2 1 14 15 16 17 18 19/0

Printed in China 62
First Printing, September 2014

page 15

page 67

page 25

page 34

STEP INTO THE WORLD OF RIPLEY'S

Ripley's world is truly extraordinary. When Robert Ripley began working at *The New York Globe* newspaper as a cartoonist in 1913, he made it his mission to reveal the most unbelievable stories from around the world. He used real-life stories of people and places he had seen on his travels in his cartoons.

Robert Ripley drew the first Ripley's Believe It or Not! cartoon in 1918. The cartoons are still published daily around the world, and there have been just five Ripley cartoonists since then.

By 1933, Robert Ripley was so popular that he opened his first museum, or Odditorium, to showcase all the things he had collected. People would send him their "believe it or nots!" and during the 1930s and 1940s he received more mail than Santa Claus and the US Presidents.

Robert Ripley was so famous that when he died in 1949, thousands lined the streets of New York to watch his coffin pass by. Today the Ripley collection includes 30,000 artifacts, 30,000 photos, and 125,000 cartoons.

Ripley visited more than 200 countries, traveling by plane, boat, camel, horse, and donkey!

This cartoon was drawn by Ripley's current cartoonist, John Graziano, who initially sent in his drawings to Ripley's as a teenager before getting the job.

Ripley's has just opened a brand-new aquarium in Toronto, Canada, featuring the longest underwater moving walkway of its kind in North America.

The Ripley's team continues to hunt for the best "believe it or nots!" from around the world today. Using many different sources, including our website, YouTube, Facebook, Twitter, mail, TV, and radio shows, as well as sending out researchers to find stories, we are forever gathering the best of the best for our Ripley fans.

"I made a living out of the fact that truth is stranger than fiction."

ROBERT RIPLEY

There are 31 Ripley's Believe It or Not! Odditoriums in nine different countries around the world. This one is in Niagara Falls, Canada.

WHAT'S NEW IN RIPLEY'S WORLD?

Ripley's archivist Edward Meyer, based in Ripley's head office in Orlando, Florida, is always looking for artifacts for the Ripley's Believe It or Not! Odditoriums. Here are just a few of the amazing exhibits he has bought this year. Sometimes the exhibits find him, and sometimes he finds them. . . .

This portrait of John Lennon from The Beatles was made using puzzle pieces by artist Doug Powell from Florida. Ripley's bought the piece after Doug took it to Ripley's HQ.

This sculpture of the Hulk is made entirely out of car parts and weighs two tons! Edward was in Thailand hunting for exhibits when he discovered this fantastic piece.

Edward bought this bike made from roadkill bones by artist Rasha "Reese" Moore from Florida, after Rasha took it to the Ripley's "Bizarre Buying Bazaar" in July 2013.

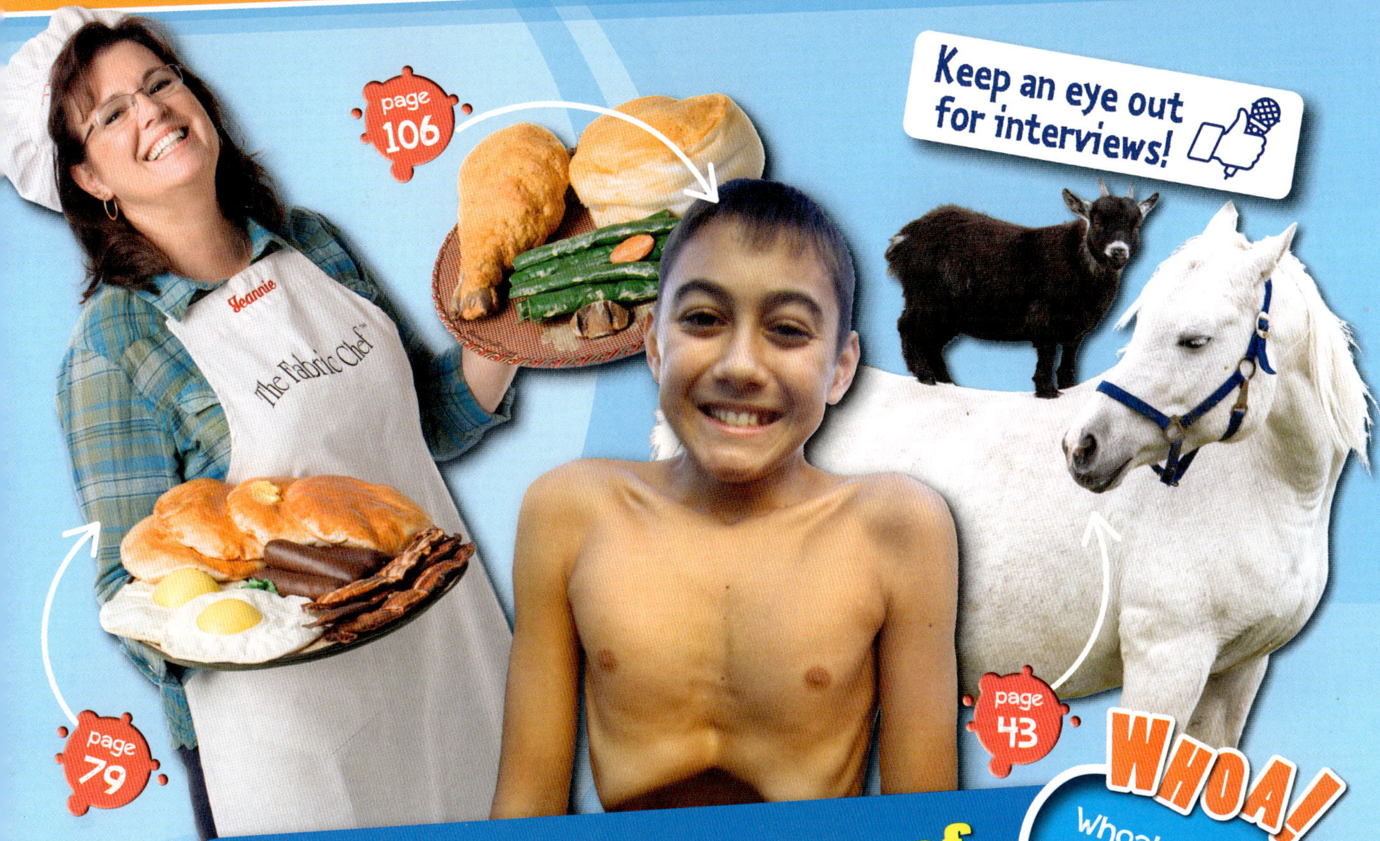

Keep an eye out for interviews!

page 106

page 79

page 43

WHOA!

Whoa! Bet you didn't know these facts!

You won't believe some of these amazing stories . . .

We feature stories sent in by you! Check out the believe it or nots! above. They submitted their pictures and are now part of this year's Ripley's book!

If you have a story you think Ripley's would like, get in touch!

Visit our website: **www.ripleybooks.com**

E-mail us: **bionresearch@ripleys.com**

Follow us: **Facebook, Twitter, and Pinterest**

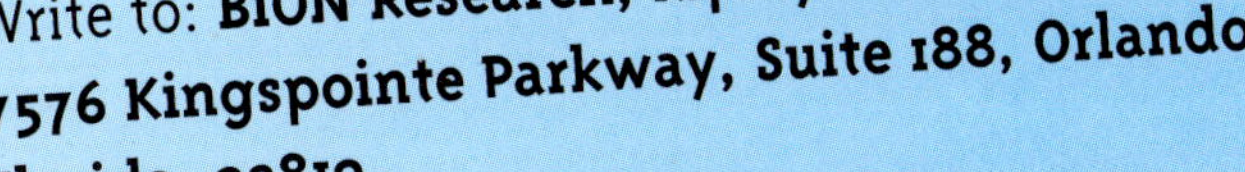

Write to: **BION Research, Ripley Entertainment Inc., 7576 Kingspointe Parkway, Suite 188, Orlando, Florida, 32819**

Ripley's Believe It or Not!

Download our app for free!

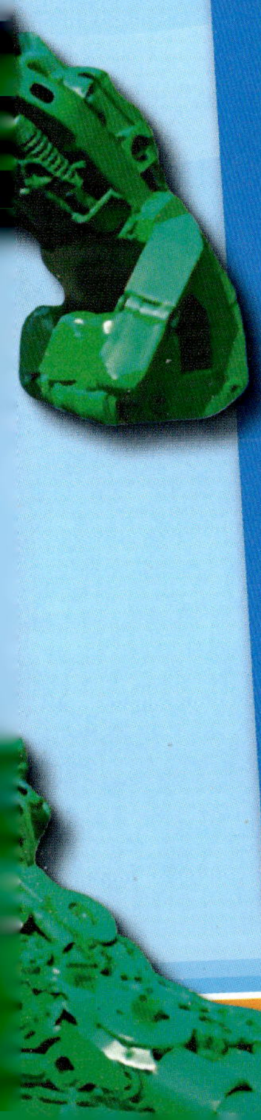

1

SUPERPOWERS

DON'T LOOK DOWN

STRIKE A POSE

Slovenian climber Martina Cufar started practicing yoga to help her focus when climbing. Therefore, it seemed right that she should try it out after scaling this 11,500-foot peak in the French Alps. Martina posed on the four-foot-square top of a rock overlooking Mont Blanc.

DEATH-DEFYING PLUNGE

These images have been blended together to show the cliff divers of Acapulco, Mexico, as they plunge from the 125-foot cliffs at La Quebrada into the Pacific Ocean. The sea below can be from 6 to 16 feet deep depending on the waves, so timing is vital to make sure they land in deep-enough water.

Hitting the High Notes

A trio of daredevil musicians, calling themselves Led Zipline after the 1970s' British rock band Led Zeppelin, played to a small audience as they dangled from a rope 1,000 feet above the Gorges du Verdon—France's answer to the Grand Canyon. Singer Mich Kemeter, didgeridoo player Armin Holzer, and guitarist Niccolò Zarattini serenaded Mich's girlfriend, Karine, and mountaineering photographer Alexandre Buisse.

WHOA!

Daredevil Rob Roy Collins successfully escaped from a straitjacket while suspended headfirst 60 feet in the air—from the tracks of a roller coaster!

TOUGH JOB

CLOSE TO THE EDGE

This excavator driver had little room to maneuver as he demolished a 12-story hotel from the top down. The excavator was lifted to the top of the narrow, triangular building in the Chinese city of Taiyuan by a 500-ton crane.

MAJOR MAINTENANCE JOB

Each year, 105 gallons of metal cleaner are used to clean France's famous Eiffel Tower, while every seven years, 25 painters spend 15 months repainting the Paris landmark. They use 66 tons of paint in three shades of brown—the lightest at the top, and the darkest at the bottom.

COLOSSAL COIN COLLECTION

A family who ran a tofu shop in eastern China arrived at their bank with more than a quarter of a ton in small change that they had collected over 30 years. Bank staff members worked for five days to count the coins, which were worth about $7,500.

JAWS OF DEATH

Greg Parker, owner of Australia's Ballarat Wildlife Park and dad of the amazing Charlie Parker on page 41, raised this 700-pound saltwater crocodile named Gator from a hatchling. He noticed that Gator often jumped around in his pool so he trained him to jump up to grab his food—and give visitors a glimpse of his fearsome teeth.

AGAINST THE ODDS

DAREDEVIL DIVER

As if plunging from a high diving board into a pool just nine feet deep is not tricky enough, Nicholas Saurey makes the leap while engulfed in flames. Once lit, the French daredevil says he waits until he gets too hot and then jumps.

SUPER SKIER

Show skier Julian Carr performed a heart-stopping flip from a 66-foot-high mountain ledge before landing on his back in the snow. The professional skier dropped headfirst from the sheer cliff in Utah without suffering a single injury, leaving a trail of snow behind him.

Inspirational Iron Girl

When Winter Vinecki's father died from prostate cancer, the young triathlete and national IronKids champion set up the Team Winter organization to raise money to fight the disease. Winter, from Salem, Oregon, has run marathons on all seven continents at only 14 years old and plans to compete in the 2018 Winter Olympics as an aerial skier. Between sports commitments, the grade-A student gives talks to encourage other kids to lead active lives.

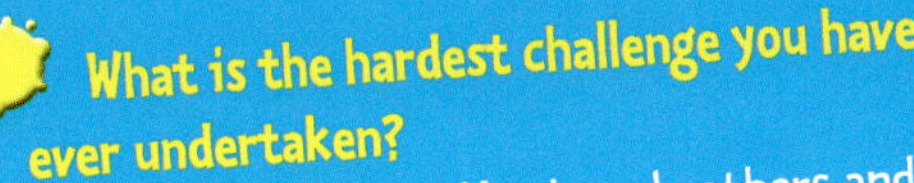

When did you start competing and why?
I was just five years old, and used to travel with my mom and dad to triathlons they would compete in. They had a triathlon at St. Joseph Island, Canada, for kids and I wanted to try it, and I have loved it ever since. Now, I also compete in running and aerial skiing.

What is the hardest challenge you have ever undertaken?
It was losing my dad. My three brothers and I were very young when we lost him, and it was the toughest challenge I had to face. All the other challenges were still difficult, but even if they hurt, I know my dad never gave up when he was fighting cancer, so I never give up.

What has been your favorite challenge?
I really enjoyed the 2013 marathon tour, as I got to visit lots of different countries. Peru was my favorite, even though it is the hardest marathon in the world. It took nine hours to complete! But I won that race.

GREAT HEIGHTS

Frenchman Alain Robert scaled the 2,716-foot Burj Khalifa in Dubai—the tallest building in the world—without a harness.
In 1876, Maria Spelterini became the first woman to cross Niagara Falls on a high wire.
Jordan Romero climbed the peaks of the highest mountain on every continent, all before he turned 16.
Nik Wallenda battled wind and sand as he walked across a two-inch-thick steel cable suspended 1,500 feet above the Little Colorado River Gorge near the Grand Canyon, Arizona. The high-wire artist, who is from a family of wirewalkers, completed the quarter-of-a-mile walk without a safety harness.
WHOA!
Chinese tightrope walker Adili Wuxor walked over two tightrope artists who were lying down on a 300-foot-high wire across the Pearl River in Ghangzhou Province in 2013.

SO BRAVE!

POWERFUL PYTHON

When tour guide Tommy Owen spotted a Burmese python in the Florida Everglades, he grabbed the snake—only to find it was ten feet long. The python wrapped itself around his arm, but Tommy and a fellow guide managed to overpower it.

Shark conservationist Ocean Ramsey swims with sharks without any protection in an attempt to prove they are not as fearsome as people think.

JAW-DROPPING ACT

Ukrainian lion tamer Oleksiy Pinko risks death as he dances with a lion before opening the big cat's jaws and putting his head inside its mouth. In 2010, the circus performer had a lucky escape when two lions unexpectedly pounced on him, injuring his arm.

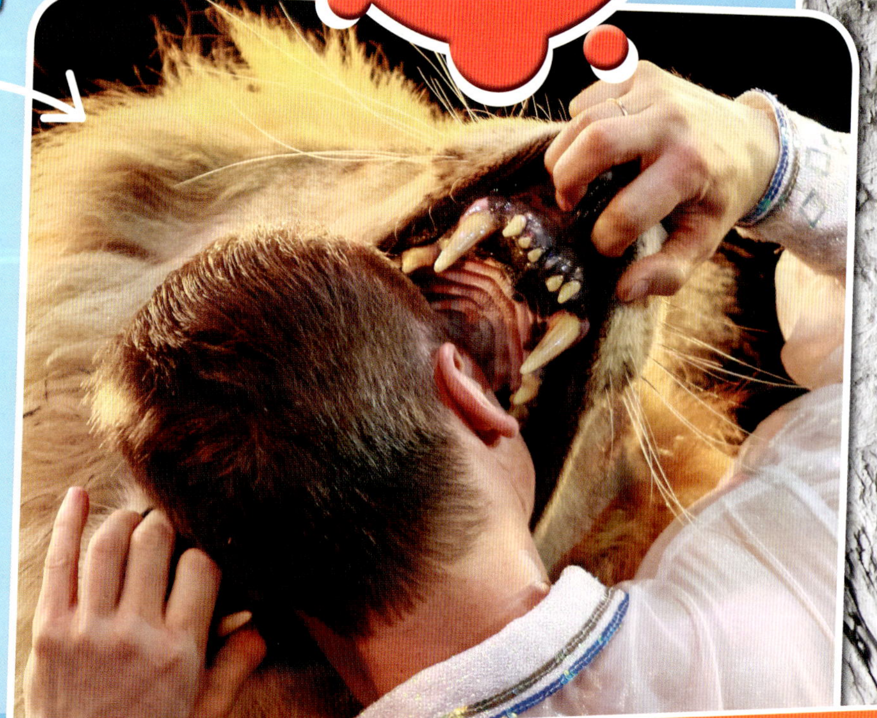

Thrill-seeking photographer Sam Bié dangled from a rock face to get this shot of Spanish climber Dani Andrada scaling "The Great Arch." The huge limestone rock in the Getu Valley, in China's Guizhou Province, is 525 feet high, 230 feet wide, and 449 feet long. Sam, from southern France, climbed for an hour to get into position opposite the arch so he could capture the amazing image.

TO THE LIMIT

In August 2012, 138 skydivers flew at speeds of 220 mph, in tight formation, upside down, over northern Illinois.

INCREDIBLE FEAT

Qi Xixiang is seen here pulling a fighter plane using just one ear. The Chinese stunt artist has been performing feats of strength using his ears for about 20 years. He managed to pull the four-ton plane more than 30 feet at a show in Tianjin, China.

OUCH!

"Iron Queen" Asha Rani pulled a 13-ton bus over 56 feet with her hair.

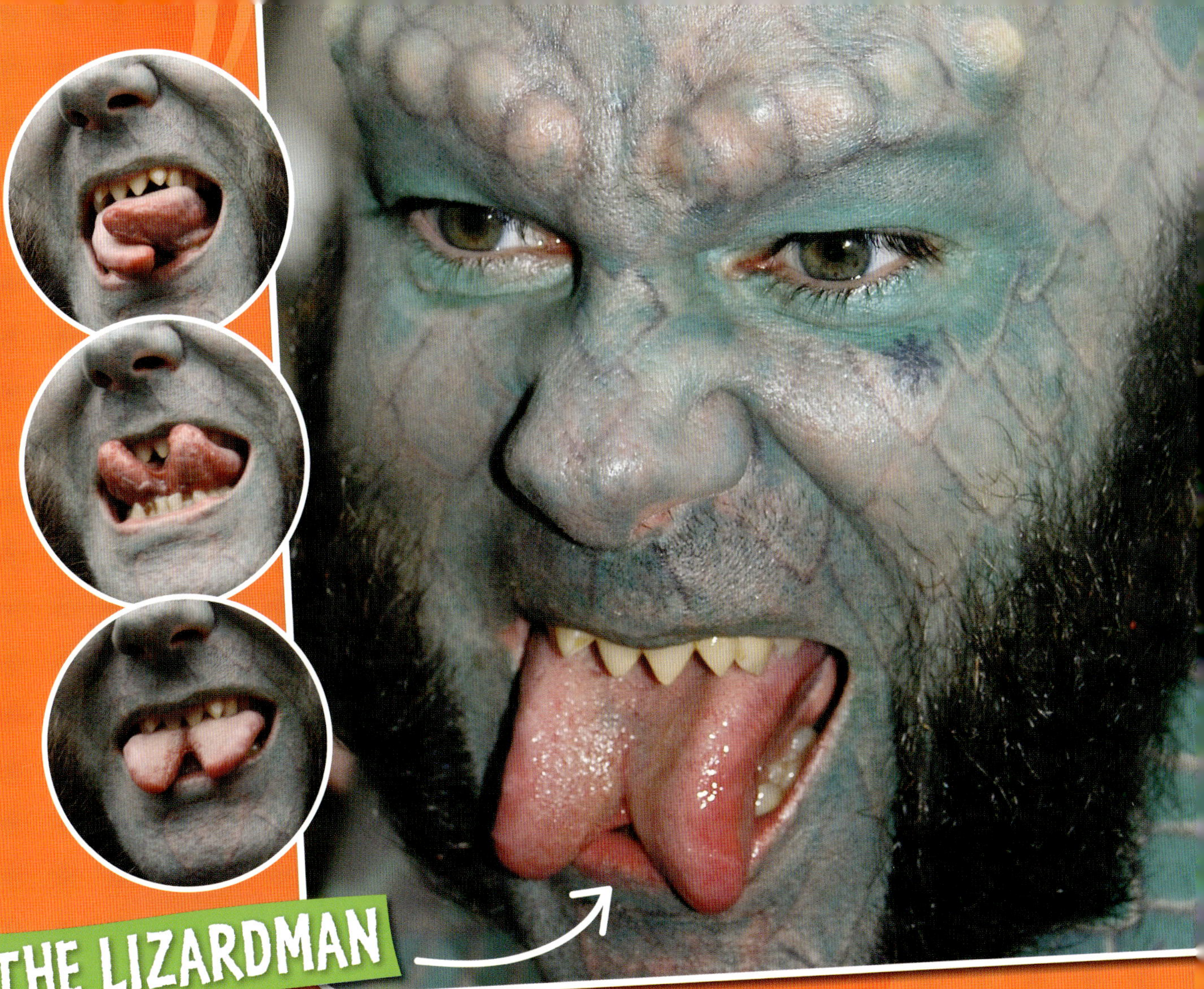

THE LIZARDMAN

Erik Sprague from Austin, Texas, has spent years transforming himself into Lizardman. He has spent 700 hours being tattooed, has four of his teeth filed into sharp crocodile-like fangs, and five Teflon horns implanted over each eye. His tongue has also been split into two! Erik performs sideshow stunts, such as sword-swallowing, fire breathing, and threading a metal corkscrew through his nose and mouth.

WHOA!

Erik says he finds it hard to eat apples because when he tries to bite them his sharp teeth simply tear off thin strips.

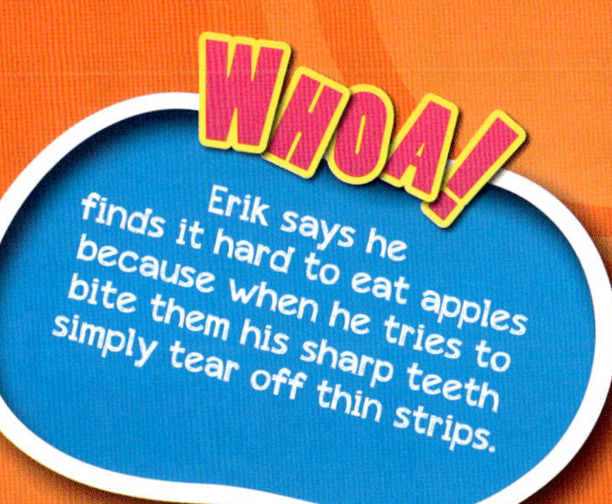

GOING THE DISTANCE

CORNFLAKE QUEST

English cereal lover Mick Hobday has spent ten years and $57,000 traveling to 63 countries in search of the perfect cornflake. He has crunched his way through 4,000 bowls of foreign flakes with milk and sugar. He is pictured here in Mauritania, where he said the camel milk tasted awful.

TUK TUK TRAVELERS

British teachers Nick Gough and Richard Sears are driving around the world in a tuk tuk to promote education. They set off from London's British Museum in 2012 and have so far traveled through Europe, Africa, and Asia in the three-wheeled rickshaw, which has a downhill speed of only 34 mph.

EXTREME IRONER

Teenage boys rarely take an interest in household chores, but an extreme ironing calendar inspired 17-year-old Kevin Krupitzer to seek out weird places to iron. His bizarre locations include a roof, a canoe, and this remote rock near his hometown of Gilbert, Arizona.

LONG-DISTANCE ROAD TRIPPERS

Herman and Candelaria Zapp left Argentina in their 1928 vintage car in 2000, and have since traveled almost 200,000 miles and visited more than 44 countries. Along the way, Candelaria has given birth to four children, each one born in a different country.

CHILD'S PLAY

SPEEDY SLIDE

The Insano waterslide in Brazil towers over the Atlantic Ocean, but thrill seekers have little time to enjoy the view as the ride takes less than five seconds. The slide is as tall as a 14-story building, and riders reach speeds of up to 65 mph as they plummet down.

RIDING HIGH

The Eclipse swing carousel in Stockholm, Sweden, is not for the fainthearted. Riders sit with their legs dangling nearly 400 feet up in the air, suspended from eight-foot chains. Those with a head for heights are rewarded with panoramic views of the city as they spin around at 44 mph.

Splash Down

Darren Taylor, aka Professor Splash, emerged red-faced after diving into a pool of tomato sauce just 12 inches deep from a 26-foot-high platform. Spectators donned plastic ponchos to avoid getting splattered as the professional shallow diver, from Denver, Colorado, performed the stunt in Sydney, Australia. He said that the jump was the most difficult in his 25-year career.

The first ketchup didn't have any tomatoes in it! It came from China and was originally made of fish and herbs.

HEAT OF THE MOMENT...

Stuntman Steve Hudis jumped over 15 motorcycles and through a giant fireball in a school bus before landing safely.
The Tinstix of Dynamite display team thrilled crowds at the International Airshow in Melbourne, Australia, with their combination of state-of-the-art pyrotechnics and precision aerobatics. US stunt pilots Skip Stewart and Melissa Pemberton, and pyrotechnic wizard Rich Gibson, made sure that the show went off with a bang.
David "The Bullet" Smith Jr. has been shot out of cannons over 5,000 times and has traveled as far as 200 feet.
Motorcycle stuntman Dennis Pinto set himself on fire, drove into a van, and flipped over it before landing safely on the other side.
WHOA!
Steve Truglia from London, England, performed a card trick while his body was on fire in flames hot enough to melt tin. Firefighters extinguished the flames when he had finished.

UM, ARE YOU SURE?

LEAP OF FAITH

Adrenaline addict Paul Morton is seen here jumping backward off the top of the 1,380-foot-tall Kuala Lumpur Tower in Malaysia. The BASE jumper (who jumps off buildings using a parachute to break his fall) from New Zealand joined other professionals from 18 countries to take part in the annual International Tower Jump.

VIEWS TO DIE FOR

These daring tourists are inching their way along one of the most dangerous hiking trails in the world. The treacherous Chang Kong Cliff Road on the edge of China's Huashan Mountain is just 12 inches wide. It offers spectacular views—if anyone is brave enough to turn around and look.

Going for the Burn

Commuters were shocked to see a man in a straitjacket hanging upside down from a burning rope attached to the London Eye, a famous Ferris Wheel. Jonathan Goodwin had just minutes to escape as he dangled 200 feet above the river Thames. As his straitjacket caught fire, the British escapologist struggled free with just seconds to spare. His past stunts include being buried alive and being attacked by sharks.

How did you come up with the idea for the stunt?
Ever since I was seven years old I have been fascinated by the feats of famous daredevils like the escape artist Harry Houdini. One of Houdini's most famous feats was escaping from a straitjacket while hanging hundreds of feet up in the air from a public landmark. I have always wanted to attempt this stunt, but wanted to update it for a modern audience, so I decided to also set the rope on fire!

Did you feel nervous during the stunt?
Ironically, I am not the biggest fan of heights, so stepping to the edge of the capsule and seeing the drop was pretty intense. I have some mental processes that I go through when doing a stunt, which allow me to focus on the task at hand, and not get scared or overwhelmed.

Have you ever had any near misses?
I had a seriously close shave when free solo-climbing a skyscraper in central London. A squall came in when I was just 20 feet from the top, and the gusting wind felt like it was going to pull me off the building. Thankfully, I made it, but I don't think I have ever been as relieved to finish a climb.

2

CURIOUS CREATURES

LOOK AT ME!

APPLE-LOVING APE

If an apple a day keeps the doctor away, this orangutan at the Moscow Zoo in Russia must want to avoid the doctor for the whole week! After tossing the fruit into the air like balls, the great ape stuffed seven apples into his mouth at once.

SPIDER HAT

Spiders often carry their babies on their backs, but this youngster has hitched a ride on its mother's head. The mini-me spider hat probably keeps her dry, but they make a daunting double act for anyone who is scared of spiders. The gruesome twosome was captured on camera in Batam, Indonesia.

CROSS-EYED KITTY

Spangles the cross-eyed cat has his own Facebook page with more than 37,000 likes. The famous feline became an Internet sensation after his owner, Mary Buchanan from South Carolina, posted photos of him wearing quirky costumes, including a pirate outfit and a jester's hat.

WHOA!

When a woman walked into her house in West Vancouver, Canada, she was very surprised to find a bear in her kitchen eating porridge! She called the police, and it took three officers to remove the bear safely.

ONE OF A KIND

Some people think zebras are black with white stripes, while others say they are white with black stripes. Whatever the truth, each pattern is unique—and none more so than this zebra with spots on its back. The unusual creature was discovered in the Masai Mara, Kenya.

HUMAN CONTACTS

SWEATER-LOVING PARROT

British bird charity worker Rebecca Blagg nursed a neglected parrot named Charlie back to health after he plucked out all his feathers. Rebecca knitted a parrot-sized sweater to keep Charlie warm, and now he squawks and stamps if she tries to take it off.

WHOA!

A pet parakeet that escaped near Tokyo, Japan, was returned to his owner after he was handed over to the police and told them his address.

PIG IN THE CITY

Ziggy J. Piggy would rather get his snout into hot milk drinks at his local coffee shop than root around in mud down on the farm. His owner, Jan Leader from Queensland, Australia, takes the miniature pig everywhere she goes and says he loves city life and trips to the beach.

Burglars Beware

Like most pet cats, Enzo loves sleeping on his owner's bed, scratching the furniture, and jumping onto the kitchen counter. The difference is that Enzo is a 375-pound Bengal tiger! Michael Jamison from South Africa bought Enzo after burglars targeted his home—and, as if one giant house cat is not enough, he has recently adopted a second big cat, a young Siberian tiger named Ozzy.

TAKE FLIGHT

Starlings often join forces to form huge flocks, especially when a predator is nearby. When these birds spotted a peregrine falcon at an English nature reserve, they took to the air in a swirling formation that morphed into the shape of a giant bird—more than enough to scare any predator away.

WHOA!

In December 2011, sadly, thousands of birds were either killed or injured after crashing headfirst into parking lots and snow-covered fields in Utah. The flock mistook the snow for water.

MINDS OF THEIR OWN

WHAT A FLUKE!

A pelican had a lucky escape when it dove down to catch a fish in Port San Luis Harbor, California, and ended up in the mouth of a huge humpback whale. Luckily, humpbacks are filter feeders and only eat tiny fish and shellfish, so it soon spat the bird out again.

SLAM DUNK

This dolphin could give professional basketball players a lesson as he performs the perfect dunk with his nose. The clever creature was shooting some hoops at a dolphin sanctuary in Cuba when this photo was taken by Sergio Longhi from Slovenia.

STRANGE NEST SITE

Commuters in the English city of Leicester were surprised to find a mistle thrush nesting between the red and yellow signals at a busy intersection. Mistle thrushes are known for their untidy nests containing odd materials. This nest includes pieces of ribbon.

WHOA!

Retired racehorse Lukas became a star all over the world by learning to recognize different shapes, identifying numbers, and to sit and fetch like a dog.

TAKING THE PLUNGE

A farmer in Hunan Province, central China, has trained his pigs to dive because he believes that it makes them healthier, and he can therefore sell them for more money. Huang Deming's pigs dive into a pond from a ten-foot-high board at least three times a day.

MAN'S BEST FRIENDS

FELINE FANATIC

British cat breeder Marlene Howes has dedicated her life to her prize-winning feline friends and admits that she would do anything for her cats. She has a total of 40 and spends more than $1,000 a month feeding and caring for them.

JUST WALKING THE SHEEP

When Wally the lamb was orphaned, volunteer shepherd Wolfgang Grensens from Lübeck, northern Germany, decided to adopt the six-week-old baby. Wally has since become one of the family and goes for walks on a leash alongside Wolfgang's three Australian cattle dogs.

Rookie Ranger

Three-year-old Charlie Parker is Australia's youngest wildlife ranger. Charlie comes from a long line of animal experts and has grown up at the Ballarat Wildlife Park in Victoria, where his playmates are snakes and North American alligators. The park is also home to more cuddly companions, including wombats and koalas, but the fearless preschooler prefers to swim alongside the alligators and handle Pablo, the eight-foot-long boa constrictor.

CANINE CARNIVAL

Twice a year, dogs and dog lovers flock to Toronto, Canada, to attend Woofstock, a canine festival featuring fashion shows, agility tests, costume competitions, and a stupid-trick contest. Yorkshire terrier Remy, seen here with his owner, made the final of the best-dressed dog competition.

The Basenji dog breed is not able to bark.

Dolphins can swim and sleep at the same time.

GOAT RIDER

Goats are great climbers, so when Sunshine the horse lies down, one of the pygmy goats that lives on Angie Power's farm in the Canadian province of Newfoundland and Labrador will often climb onto her back. When Sunshine walks away, the goat is happy to stay aboard for the ride.

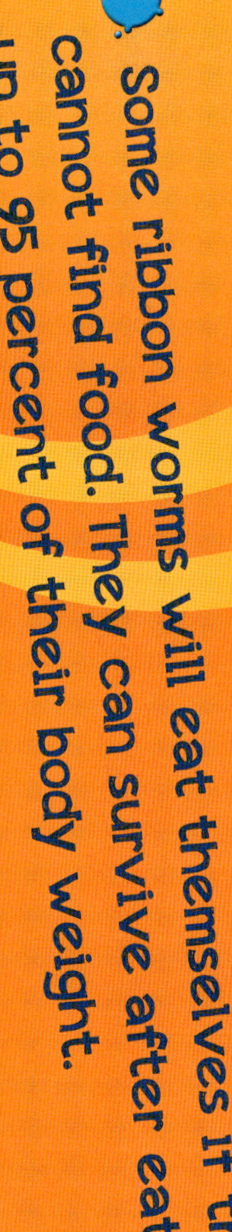

WHOA!

A prize ewe in Shropshire, England, gave birth to quintuplets—five lambs—at odds of one in a million. Each tiny lamb weighed just over three pounds.

CREATURES OF STRANGE HABIT

BUFFALO BOAT

This dog is taking quite a risk as it sits on top of a water buffalo wallowing in the Ravi River in Lahore, Pakistan. Most animals keep clear of these massive, powerful beasts, which are armed with sharp horns and can weigh more than 2,000 pounds.

CHEEKY CHIPMUNK

As Richard Bishop from Toronto, Canada, was eating peanuts outside a friend's house, a greedy chipmunk picked up the scent. The chipmunk grabbed as many nuts as possible and stuffed them into its cheek pouches before running away to hide them and returning for more.

HOUSE PONIES

Heidi Northover and her daughter Corinna, from Derby, England, allow their miniature ponies free rein inside their home. Pint-sized ponies Roanie, Star, and Hania watch TV in the living room, drink water straight from the kitchen faucet, and nibble carrots from the vegetable rack.

MOP MOM

Staff at a wildlife rescue center in Somerset, England, had a bright idea when six orphaned baby owls kept climbing all over one another looking for warmth and shelter. They gave the owlets a colorful surrogate mom in the shape of a mop head that mimics their mother's wings.

CREEPY CRAWLIES

For every human on Earth, there are 1.5 billion bugs.
Donald Jusa, who works as a geologist in East Kalimantan, Indonesia, captured this stunning image of an insect's head by holding the camera just one inch away from his subject. It shows the many lenses in the insect's bulging eyes, which enable it to see all around its body.
Tarantulas can survive without food for more than two years.
Some wasps sleep (and even hibernate for months) while hanging by their teeth.
WHOA!
Chinese beekeepers Li Wenhua and Yan Hongxia invited thousands of bees to their wedding. They attracted them by planting queen bees on their clothes.

CUDDLY COMPANIONS

PRICKLY PALS

When an animal rescue center in eastern England offered a home to a rare albino African pygmy hedgehog, they were unsure whether their resident black-and-white African pygmy hedgehog would accept the new arrival. Luckily, they are now the best of friends and love to burrow together.

ULTIMATE SHEEPDOG

Sheep farmers rely on their dogs to help out with the flock and Jess the springer spaniel does more work than most. She loves to carry things in her mouth, so she has been trained to bottle-feed the orphaned lambs on a farm in southwest England.

SPECIAL BOND

Russian veterinary student Andrey Golosov hand-reared a cheetah named Seva for five months after the cub was rejected by his mother. The cheetah was returned to the Moscow Zoo and is now fully grown with cubs of his own, but he still recognizes Andrey as his foster dad.

TANGLED TRUNKS

Elephants use their trunks to greet and touch one another, and they hug by wrapping their trunks together. These three African elephants spent about half an hour with their trunks entwined after they met up at the Addo Elephant National Park in South Africa.

TO THE RESCUE

FRIEND IN NEED

Dotty the donkey was awarded a prize for animal bravery after rushing to the aid of her stablemate Stanley the sheep when he was attacked by a dog at a farm in England. Dotty pinned the dog to the ground, then bit it on the back until it let go of Stanley and ran away.

Hippo Hero

Hippos are one of Africa's deadliest animals, but this adult male showed his softer side when he came to the aid of an injured wildebeest. The unfortunate animal was part of a huge herd traveling across the Masai Mara in Kenya to reach new feeding grounds. As they jostled to cross the Masai River, it fell down a 15-foot bank into the water and got stuck on a rock.

1 A wildebeest falls and gets stuck on a rock....

CLOSE CALL

A baby squirrel found itself in an unstable position after falling from a woodpecker's nest in Pittsburgh, Pennsylvania. It was left dangling from a thin branch 25 feet above the ground. Luckily, its mom sprang to the rescue and grabbed hold of the baby's tail.

WHOA!

Ha Wenjin gave up her job and sold her house to adopt and look after more than 1,500 stray dogs at her rescue center in Nanjing, China.

2 A hippo approaches the creature . . .

3 . . . and manages to pull the wildebeest free.

OUT OF PLACE!

OUT OF THIS WORLD!

WONDER OF NATURE

In summer, the Spotted Lake, in British Columbia, looks like a giant artist's palette. The lake, which lies in one of Canada's hottest regions, is full of minerals, and as the water evaporates, they are all left behind. Large "spots" made up of the various minerals appear in different colors, leaving hardened paths around them.

FIERY PEAK

Mount Grinnell, in Glacier National Park, Montana, looks as if it is glowing red hot in this picture, taken at sunrise by photographer Harry Lichtman. The sun broke through the clouds for a few minutes and bathed the reddish-brown rock in a warm, orange light.

ODD ICE

These strange, frosted disks are natural ice forms, which are created when pieces of ice rub together in strong winds and the edges are rounded off. It is called pancake ice and was photographed on the surface of Lake Onega in northwest Russia.

BLOODRED SEA

Visitors to beaches in Sydney, Australia, must have thought there had been a massive shark attack when they discovered that the sea had turned bloodred. The rare phenomenon, which lasted for several days, was caused by a huge bloom of algae (tiny plants).

TRAVEL NEWS

LUXURY LOCKUP

A jail is probably the last place you would choose to spend the night, but Het Arresthuis in the Netherlands has gourmet cuisine, DVD players, flat-screen TVs, and a sauna. The former penitentiary has been transformed into a luxurious hotel where the guests are happy to be doing time.

CLASSIC CAMPER

Fans of the classic VW camper can relive the 1960s in this full-size canvas replica. The tent can sleep four people in two rooms, and although it may not get you very far, it is guaranteed not to break down on the freeway.

COUGH

Zzzz

EGG-CARTON SPITFIRE

The Imperial War Museum in eastern England is home to many World War II planes, but none like the fighter created by Charlotte Austen and Jack Munro to raise money for a military charity, Eggs for Soldiers. Their life-size Spitfire is made from 6,500 egg cartons, 1.3 gallons of glue, 5,000 nails, and 10,000 staples.

WHOA!

Diggerland is a group of theme parks filled with diggers! The parks, based in the UK, have rides such as the dig-a-round and let older kids race in dump trucks and dig for buried treasure in a digger.

HUMAN TORTOISE

Liu Lingchao travels around Guangxi Province, China, collecting and selling recyclable bottles. He walks about 12 miles a day, and wherever he goes, his house goes with him. His hut is made of bamboo and plastic sheets and weighs about 130 pounds.

FRUITS OF THE FOREST

TERRIFYING TREE

With its staring eyes, curling tongue, and green drool spilling from its mouth, this tree looks as if it belongs in a theme park. Instead, it stands on the grounds of a nursing home in eastern England. The tree reminded the photographer of Edvard Munch's famous painting *The Scream*.

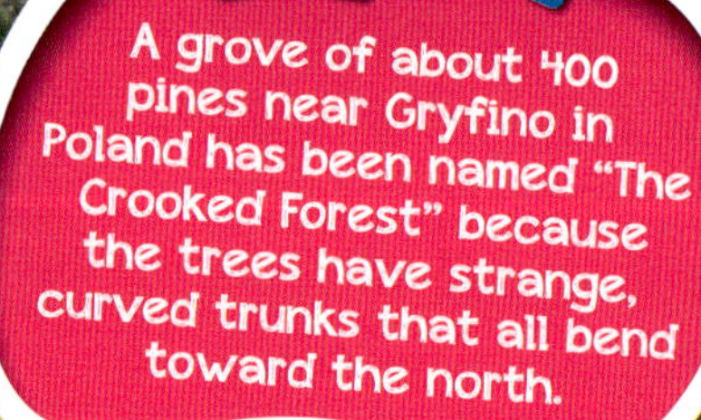

BIG CHOP

Before modern machinery was available, it took a gang of lumberjacks a week to fell a redwood tree. This photo, taken in Humboldt County, California, in about 1915, shows men using axes and handsaws to work their way through one towering giant. The massive trunks were later hauled away by teams of oxen.

Mushroom Masterpieces

Corey Corcoran from Boston, Massachusetts, takes his inspiration from nature when he creates these detailed etchings on Artist's Conk mushrooms. The fungus gets its name because it is possible to draw on the surface with any sharp object. Corey has just 48 hours to complete his work before the fungus hardens, and there is no room for mistakes because they are impossible to erase.

About 50 to 70 volcanoes erupt each year, mostly under the sea.

SUPERCHARGED STROLLER

British plumber Colin Furze has given his son's buggy a boost by adding a motorcycle engine. An accelerator and brake levers control the speed, and there is even space for his shopping purchases. The stroller can reach 50 mph, but Colin doesn't travel at that speed with the baby on board.

LITTLE LANDSCAPES

Steve Wheen is a gardener with no garden, so he creates mini landscapes in some of Britain's two million potholes to highlight the state of the country's roads. Steve has created more than 150 miniature gardens on the streets of London, including a tiny golf course and cricket- and tennis-themed plots.

WHOA!

No one has ever seen the "sailing stones" in Death Valley, California, move, but there is clear evidence that the rocks, which can weigh hundreds of pounds, have traveled up to 700 feet.

The Mall of America, located in Bloomington, Minnesota, is so big that it can hold 24,336 school buses.

MOVING IN?

WHAT A DUMP!

German artist Ha Schult has built a five-bedroom hotel covered with garbage collected from European beaches and waste dumps. Beach Garbage Hotel, in the Spanish capital of Madrid, is designed to draw tourists' attention to the amount of trash that is dumped in the ocean.

MADE OF CHOCOLATE!

SWEET SHOWROOM

This room made of chocolate was unveiled at a shopping mall in Minsk, Belarus. Sculptor Elena Kliment used more than 1,300 pounds of chocolate to make everything from the chairs to the flowers and teacups. Her melt-in-the-mouth masterpiece was later broken up and shared with visitors.

SEASONED TRAVELERS

The walls and furniture in Bolivia's Palacio de Sal are made entirely of salt. About one million blocks of salt were used to build the hotel, which lies at the edge of the world's largest salt flats. Guests are politely asked not to lick the walls.

MINI MANSIONS

If you need a space—or even a street—to call your own, these top-of-the-line playhouses might fit the bill. A company in Pennsylvania is selling luxury playhouses, along with everything you need to create your own Main Street, including a fire station, diner, bank, post office, and beauty parlor.

A huge underground river runs underneath the Nile, in Egypt, with six times more water than the river above.

You might think this photo shows plumes of smoke rising from the water, but in fact they are huge swarms of lake flies emerging from Lake Malawi in southeast Africa. The insect feast attracts birds and fish—as well as local people, who squash the flies together to make patties, which they fry and eat.

The very rare occurrence of upward lightning sends electrons streaming from the ground upward, producing an electrical current and a bright streak of light.

Twice a year, the Atlantic tides meet at the mouth of the Amazon River in Brazil, creating the longest wave on Earth, up to 186 miles.

FLY FEAST!

WHOA!

In 2001, red, yellow, green, and black rain fell on the Indian state of Kerala. The rains were colored by airborne cells from local algae.

QUITE A SIGHT

Towering Tree House

In 1993, minister Horace Burgess believed he heard a message from God telling him that if he built a tree house, he would never run out of wood—and so far he hasn't. The minister's giant tree house is located just outside Crossville, Tennessee. It is currently 97 feet tall, with ten stories, 80 rooms, a spiral staircase, a basketball court, a church, and a bell tower.

CHICKEN CHURCH

People are flocking to visit a church in Tampa Bay, Florida, because it looks like a chicken. It has two eyelike, round windows above a triangular, tiled "beak." The cross on top could be compared to a crest, and the roof extends out like a pair of red wings.

WHOA!

A camouflaged box covered in mirrors, known as the Mirrorcube, is the ultimate luxury tree house. Suspended 40 feet up in the trees, it has electric heating, lighting, and working toilets!

UPSCALE HOME

Artist Howard Solomon spent 12 years building his own castle in Ona, Florida. Its walls are covered with old metal newspaper printing plates, and it has a bell tower, dungeon, and 90 stained glass windows. It also boasts a replica Spanish galleon in the moat, which is used as a restaurant.

MADE OF METAL!

WEATHER REPORT

ON A ROLL

Snow rollers, or snow donuts, are usually found on the windswept prairies of North America, rather than on the windshield of a car in eastern England. The rare, perfectly curled rolls are created by a particular combination of snow, ice, wind, temperature, and moisture.

WALL OF DUST

In spring, sandstorms are common in parts of China, as snow and ice melt and expose dry, sandy earth. This massive sandstorm hit Zhangye, in northwest China's Gansu Province, in March 2013. Eyewitnesses described it as a wall of black dust, which turned the blue sky gray.

ALIEN CLOUD

This Russian volcano looks as if it is wearing a hat, but its peak is actually hidden by a lenticular cloud. These rare clouds form when moist air passes over a mountain range. They are usually smooth and disk-shaped, which means they are often mistaken for alien spaceships.

Amazingly, a thundercloud can contain up to 300,000 tons of rain!

SMILING SKY

Freak conditions caused this upside-down rainbow, which suddenly appeared in southwest England. Normal rainbows are formed when light passes through raindrops. In this case, the sunlight bounced off ice crystals high in the sky and the light rays were reflected back up, creating a multicolored smile.

STRANGE PLACES

BEAR HUGS INCLUDED

Chinese people believe that pandas represent love, happiness, warmth, and nature, and a hotel in southwest China's Sichuan Province has been dedicated to this adorable creature. Panda-themed rooms are decorated with panda pictures, paw prints, and cuddly toys, and the staff even dress in panda costumes.

The world's longest tunnel is in the Swiss Alps and is 35 miles long.

The world's biggest building by volume is the Boeing airplane plant in Washington State—it is so large that Disneyland could fit inside!

Between 1939 and 1942, the Bahamas had an undersea post office.

When temperatures rise, many people would like a private pool, but Zhou Yuhang from Wenzhou city in China is doubly lucky. His dad has converted the back of his van into a wading pool, so the six-year-old has a pool to himself, and he can keep cool wherever he goes.

HOME, SWEET HOME

WOODEN WORLD

Italian artist Livio de Marchi has built a house where everything, inside and out, is made of wood, including the books, plates, cutlery, couches, pillows, and the clothes in the closets. He does not paint any of his sculptures because he loves the natural beauty of the wood.

SHOWER SHOW

Start each day feeling like a star. Wannabe performers dreaming of Internet fame can take center stage with this YouTube shower curtain. Your talent will be clear for all to see as you sing into the showerhead or shampoo bottle, thanks to the curtain's see-through window.

STUFF OF DREAMS

If you dream of heading into space, this duvet set based on a real astronaut's suit may be for you. Close your eyes and let the countdown begin. Meanwhile, budding princesses can dream of Prince Charming beneath a ball-gown duvet and rest their heads on a pillow with a diamond tiara.

LIGHT UP YOUR LIFE

If you're afraid of the dark or suffer from frequent power outages, bed covers and curtains that glow in the dark could be the answer. An Italian company has created a fabric called Luminex that incorporates fiber-optic cables, lit by battery-powered LEDs.

Fuyuhito Moriya built a three-story home in an area not much bigger than a parking space!

4

BREAKING BOUNDARIES

LOVE IS...

DOWN THE AISLE

Love was in the air on Valentine's Day at an IKEA store in New South Wales, Australia. Lynne Klanbida and Chad Martin adore the Swedish furniture store so much that they entered a competition to hold their wedding there. They celebrated with a cake that looked like packed-down boxes, with a wrench on top.

ROMANTIC RETREAT

Makepeace Island is the perfect romantic getaway. The 25-acre, heart-shaped island in the Noosa River, Queensland, is one of Australia's most expensive holiday resorts. The 11-room retreat is owned by Virgin Australia Airlines and comes with staff, a chef, and all-you-can-eat food.

GIVE ME A SQUEEZE

People sometimes shake a vending machine if it does not deliver the goods, but this Coca-Cola machine in Singapore asks customers for a hug in return for a free can. The company claims that the Coca-Cola Hug Me Machine is a simple idea to spread some happiness.

WHOA!

Lisa Grant and Alex Pelling are having wedding ceremonies in every country they visit. They have had 53 weddings so far. When they find their favorite place they will marry officially.

DREAM COME TRUE

Wu Conghan, aged 101, and his 103-year-old wife, Wu Sognshi, had no wedding photos because cameras were rare when they married in 1924. Therefore, they were delighted when a photographer in Sichuan Province, China, offered them a chance to re-create and record the happy day 88 years later.

CLEVER CHEFS

EDIBLE VISTA

Photographer Carl Warner has re-created the London, England, skyline using food. Tower Bridge is crafted from beans, celery, pineapple, and cereal; the London Eye ferris wheel has green bean spokes and tomato pods; and St. Paul's Cathedral has a melon dome with baby sweet corn columns.

FLYING FISH

FLYING SUSHI!

A sushi restaurant in central London, England, is trying out a new method of delivering food to customers. The flying iTray has four rotors and is controlled using an iPad. It can travel at up to 25 mph, which is six times faster than the average waiter.

High-fiber Food

Anyone tempted to take a bite from one of these tasty treats will get a shock because they have all been created from fabric. Fiber artist Jeannie Martin, from Colorado, made her first pieces of fabric food to decorate a display of china in a shop window. Since then, she has become known as "The Fabric Chef." Her recent works include giant ice cream cones and a supersized chicken dinner.

MADE OF FABRIC!

INTERVIEW

How did you come up with the idea of fabric art?
When I was in college, pop art was very popular and I really liked the idea of taking an everyday object and turning it into a great art piece. When I lived in Ridgway, Colorado, in 1997, a store owner mentioned to me that she wished she had some artificial pastries to decorate the chinaware she sold. She thought the plastic ones looked a little cheap, so I decided to make some out of fabric.

What kinds of fabrics do you use?
The best fabric is a solid-colored, low-knap flannel, but Osnaburg cotton works well for wheat rolls. And broadcloth is great for sausages!

What made you choose food as a subject?
Food can have a lot of meaning to people—good memories, parties, friends—so for me, it is like keeping those memories forever. The idea of someone wanting to eat something made of fabric is also rather fascinating. Each and every sculpture is a challenge, to make it look as real as possible.

ARTISTIC LICENSE...

New York-based artist Honey spends two hours puncturing a banana's skin with a safety pin to create portraits of her favorite celebrities.

British artist Zac Freeman creates portraits of his friends and family using trash.

Californian artist Darren Pearson uses LEDs to draw skeletal pictures in the air, in the same way that a traditional painter would use a brush. Then he captures the images using a long-exposure setting on his camera. His series of light paintings include bicycles, angels, and aliens.

French artist Michel Vienkot uses cow dung as paint to create his pictures.

WHOA!

Chen Xiang from China can write calligraphy using a brush held in his eye! He has nearly blinded himself doing it, but doctors have confirmed that his eyes are healthy.

NO SMALL FEAT

NANO-COPTER

The Nano Falcon has a wingspan smaller than a dragonfly and weighs less than half an ounce. The remote-controlled helicopter has been developed by a Japanese company using parts from smartphones. It has a range of 15 feet and flies for about five minutes on a single charge.

MINIATURE MARVELS

Dmitry Okhotsky makes tiny replicas of everyday objects, and they all work. These minute scissors can cut through paper, and a tiny vise can be tightened just like a full-sized machine. The Latvian artist uses scaled-down tools to make the micro-models from broken gadgets and trash.

TIME MACHINE

This motorcycle should run like clockwork because it is made from old watch parts. It takes artist Dan Tanenbaum from Toronto, Canada, 40 to 50 hours to build each bike, and they can sell for more than $1,000. Each one is made from parts from up to 50 watches.

FILLING THE GAP

Passersby were mystified when seven tiny houses appeared in a four-inch-wide space between two buildings in Westerstraat, Amsterdam. The house numbers in this Dutch city street jump from 54 to 70, so an advertising agency decided to fill the gap with miniature models of the seven "missing" houses.

LIGHT UP YOUR RIDE

If you are bored with your bike and want to be noticed after dark, the Monkey Light Pro can turn your spinning wheels into a piece of performance art. The LED display is visible from both sides of the bike and can be customized with your own choice of images or animations.

A team of dentists has created a 3-D toothbrush that can clean your teeth in less than six seconds. The customized brace-brush contains about 400 bristles.

The Varibike, by Martin Kraiss, allows you to pedal with both your feet and hands.

Ethan Schlussler built a 30-foot tree house but was getting tired of climbing up, so he invented a bicycle-powered elevator, allowing him to pedal up.

WHOA!

BrightFeet Slippers are new slippers with built-in lights at the front, so when you need to go to the bathroom in the middle of the night you don't need to turn the lights on!

THE LATEST THING

SELF-PAINTING DRESS

Most girls would be upset if their white dress was stained with purple ink, but that is exactly what Dutch designer Anouk Wipprecht had in mind. Her white felt, Pseudomorph dress has a sculpted neck brace that dribbles ink onto the fabric, slowly turning it purple.

ACTUALLY WAGS!

HAPPY TAIL

If you would like a new way to express your feelings, or want to know if a friend is pleased to see you, Tailly could be the answer. This Japanese invention straps around the waist and has sensors that monitor your pulse rate. The faster the heartbeat, the more the tail wags.

WHEELY ON WATER

The Panther, designed by California-based company WaterCar, can go from a car to a boat in just 15 seconds! It can be driven straight from land to water and can travel at speeds of up to 45 mph—that's nearly as fast as a speedboat!

SHOWPIECE SHOES

Kobi Levi creates shoes modeled on animals, cartoon characters, and everyday objects—including the ones shown here, based on a children's slide. One pair, featuring a ponytail and a headset mic, was inspired by Madonna's Blond Ambition tour, while his double boots were worn by Lady Gaga.

SEEING IS BELIEVING

NEVER GIVE UP!

Sameer Doshi from Illinois was determined to overcome his blindness, so he set himself the challenge of solving a Rubik's cube. It took him nine months to complete the puzzle by marking the different colors with pieces of Velcro, plastic gems, and stickers, then using his sense of touch to line them up.

ELEPHANT ENTERTAINER

Paul Barton dragged a piano up a mountain in Thailand to raise money for blind and disabled elephants living in a sanctuary near Bangkok. The British pianist, who moved to Thailand 16 years ago to be nearer to the elephants, then performed a Beethoven sonata for his oversized audience.

Blind Courage

Since losing his sight because of a rare eye condition, Dean Dunbar has completed more than 50 death-defying challenges. The extreme sports enthusiast from Scotland has bungee-jumped (right), rappelled down Britain's tallest waterfall, cliff-jumped, windsurfed, paraglided, water-skied, wingwalked, and been fired from a catapult. He is always on the lookout for new thrills and hopes to inspire other people with disabilities to try new sports.

Daniel Kish, who has been blind since he was 13 months old, can recognize a building from 1,000 feet away, after learning to interpret echoes around him.

I ♥ U

NEW BEST FRIEND

Denis the crested pigeon became attached to animal rescue volunteer Gail Daniell after she resuscitated him when he stopped breathing. Gail, from Adelaide, Australia, learned CPR during a first-aid course but never expected to use the life-saving skill on a bird.

UNUSUAL BEDMATES

A zoo owner in the Philippines celebrated the Chinese Year of the Snake in 2013 by sleeping with a bedful of snakes. The snakes are not poisonous—instead they kill by wrapping themselves around their prey and squeezing it to death, so he couldn't get too comfy with his wriggly companions.

LITTLE LOVEBIRD

Although wildlife photographer Sue Flood has seen many penguins during her long career, this emperor penguin chick was one in a million. As the chicks lose their baby plumage they develop a white patch on their chests, but this was the first time she had ever seen one shaped like a heart.

SURROGATE MOM

Two cygnets that were hatched in an incubator at Birdland Park in Gloucestershire, England, had their first swimming lesson with help from a toy swan. The baby birds would normally follow their mother into the water, so their keeper used the fluffy toy to lead them into a wading pool.

HARD TO BELIEVE

Leonardo Da Vinci never signed or dated his most famous painting, the *Mona Lisa*.

In October 2012, the Elsa-Brandstrom high school in Germany banned homework for two years!

DEFYING GRAVITY

These people appear to be scaling the walls of a townhouse, but look again and you will see that they are lying on a replica built on the ground and reflected in a giant mirror. The temporary installation in London, England, is the work of Argentinian artist Leandro Erlich.

WHOA!

Women in a village in China made the world's largest pleated skirt! It weighed 220 pounds and had a circumference of 413 feet. It was made by 999 women in 33 days.

BUDDING BRIDEZILLAS

Fifteen brides-to-be took part in a cake-eating contest in Times Square, New York, in the hope of winning $25,000 to spend on a dream wedding. The competition was held to promote the TV show *Bridezillas*, which follows the wedding preparations, and sometimes tantrums, of a group of demanding brides.

American composer John Cage composed a work in 1952 entitled "4' 33"," which consists of four minutes and 33 seconds of silence.

FILM STARS

EPIC INKING

A *Lord of the Rings* fan spent 76 hours under the needle as tattoo artist Paul McCracken, from Queensland, Australia, inked key characters from the epic trilogy onto his back. The image is a copy of a 1970s' poster drawn by British artist and musician Jimmy Cauty.

WHOA!

A museum curator spent over $32,000 on a collection of Smurfs! Karen Bell now has almost 5,000 Smurf figures and items of Smurf memorabilia from around the world.

REAL-LIFE "HOMER" CAR

Simpsons fans may remember The Homer, a car designed by Homer Simpson with a bubble dome for quarreling kids, massive cup holders, and three horns that played "La Cucaracha." Now Porcubimmer Motors, with only a $500 budget, has successfully created a real version for the 24 Hours of LeMons spoof race.

Matchstick Man

Patrick Acton spent almost three years building a model of Hogwarts School, using photographs from the *Harry Potter* movies for reference. His detailed replica contains 602,000 matchsticks stuck together with 15 gallons of glue. The career coach from Iowa has devoted thousands of hours to his hobby. His other matchstick creations include the Space Shuttle *Challenger*, New York's One World Trade Center, and the US Capitol building in Washington, DC.

5
ONE IN A MILLION

CAN YOU DO THIS?

CANNED CONTORTIONIST

You can get most things in a can nowadays—including acrobats it seems. This young performer appeared in an acrobatic show at a fair held in Ditan Park, Beijing, China, to celebrate the start of the Chinese New Year.

EXTREME OLYMPICS

India's Rural Olympics, held in Kila Raipur, attract more than 4,000 contestants from around the world. Competitors take part in extreme tests of strength and endurance, including being run over by a tractor, racing astride two galloping horses, and lifting heavy loads with their teeth.

Lengthy Locks

Five-foot-tall Cen Yingyuan is 19 inches shorter than her hair. Cen from Guigang, China, has been growing her hair for 11 years. She keeps every strand that falls out, which adds up to almost two ounces a year. Her six-foot-seven-inch locks take one hour to wash and half a day to dry.

OFFBEAT CURES

HARD TO SWALLOW

The Uyghur people from East Turkestan, which is now part of China, have been practicing traditional medicine for 2,700 years. They use remedies based on plants and animals, which are still available at street stalls today. Dried lizards and snakes are said to cure rashes, fever, and itching.

WOW!

DEEP HEAT

People in Siwa, Egypt, believe that being buried in hot sand can cure rheumatism, joint pains, and skin complaints. Patients are buried up to the neck for 20 minutes, while an attendant performs a sort of massage by walking over the sand on top of them.

WRIGGLY REMEDY

At the start of the monsoon season, around 70,000 asthma sufferers travel to Hyderabad in India to receive Bathini Fish Medicine. Patients line up to swallow a live fish, which has been stuffed with a yellow herbal paste.

WHOA!

A 17th-century medical book advised men to put chicken dung on their heads to cure baldness.

Each year, more than 30,000 pilgrims travel to Espinazo, Mexico, to visit the tomb of El Niño Fidencio, a healer who is said to have cured thousands from diseases. His followers bathe in the muddy waters of a sacred spring that they believe has healing properties.

HAIR-RAISING!

SPIDER BEARD

Chad Roberts from Richmond, Virginia, won "best in show" at the 2013 New Jersey Beard & 'Stache Competition with this beard inspired by Spider-Man. Chad uses extra-strength hairspray to style his 14-inch whiskers. His other successful beard sculptures include a bald eagle and a Christmas tree.

In ancient Rome, men often painted hair onto their bald heads.

MIGHTY MUSTACHE

Robert Ripley himself measured Arjan Desur Dangar's very long mustache at Ripley's Odditorium exhibition at the 1933 Chicago World's Fair. Before the fair, Dangar fought with his manager, who ripped off half of his mustache!

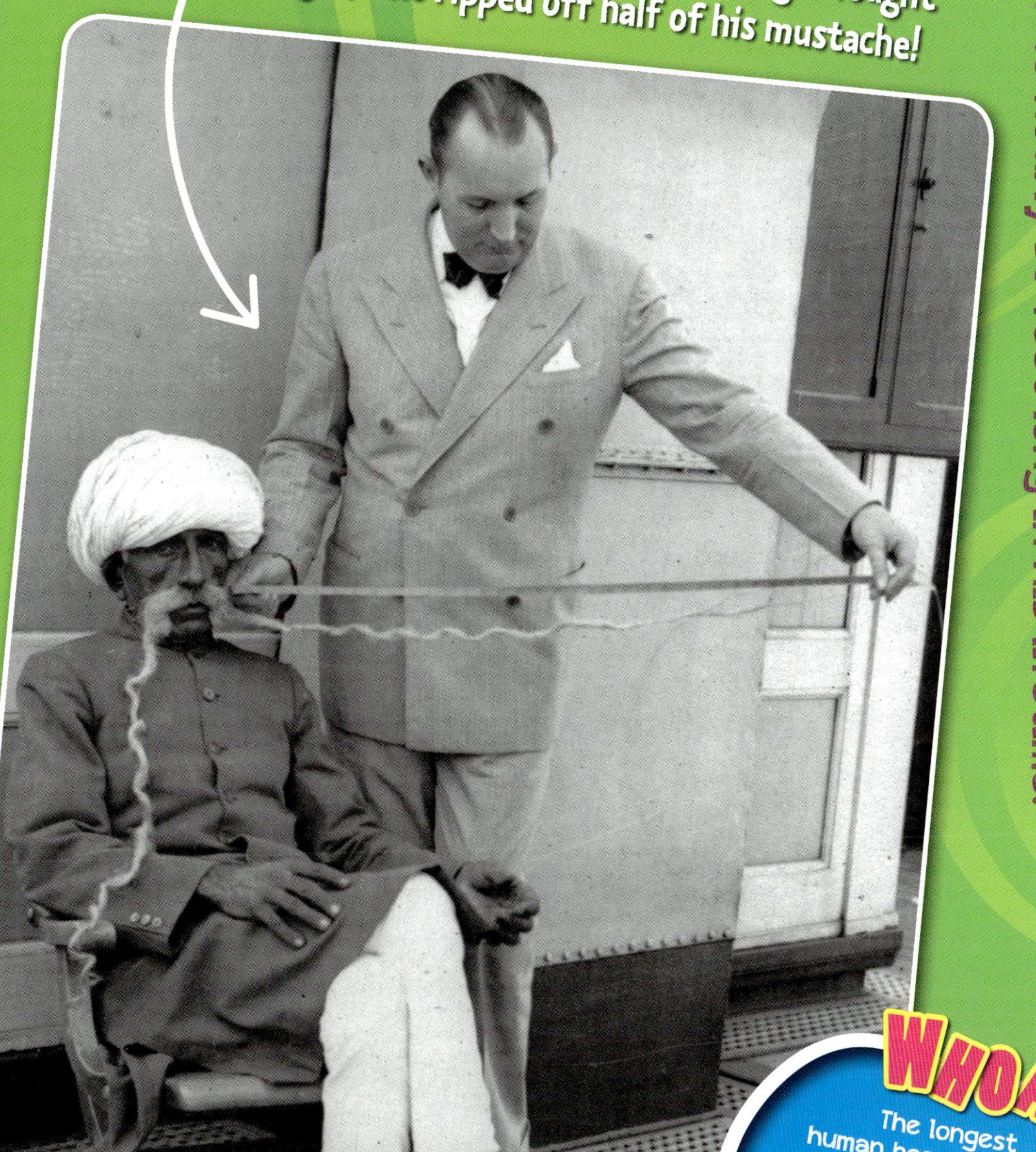

The oldest documented mustache can be found in a portrait dating back to 3,000 BC.

If the average man never trimmed his beard, it would grow to nearly 30 feet long in his lifetime.

WHOA! The longest human beard on record is 18 feet six inches. It belonged to Hans N. Langseth, who was born in Norway in 1846.

TAKE THE STRAIN

Thick Skin

Pete Tino is happy to let people walk all over him. The performer, who calls himself "The Human Floor," clearly has a high threshold when it comes to pain. He invites women to stand on him as he lies on a bed of broken glass, while his other stunts include being sandwiched between two beds of nails, eating fire, and acting as a human dartboard.

RELIGIOUS RITE

In early January, some followers of Shinto, a Japanese religion, stand in icy pools and throw buckets of freezing water over themselves as part of a cleansing ritual called misogi. The ceremony begins with warm-up exercises and special prayers.

OUCH!

ICE MAN

Hezi Dayan spent 66 hours inside an eight-ton block of ice wearing only a hat, jeans, and a T-shirt. The Israeli illusionist was sealed into the giant ice cube in Rabin Square, Tel Aviv, Israel, on December 29, 2010, and his assistants released him at midnight on New Year's Eve.

In 2008, firefighter Chris Hickman from Florida arrived at the scene of a car crash and managed to lift the damaged car about 12 inches off the ground, helping to free the trapped driver.

DON'T TRY THIS AT HOME

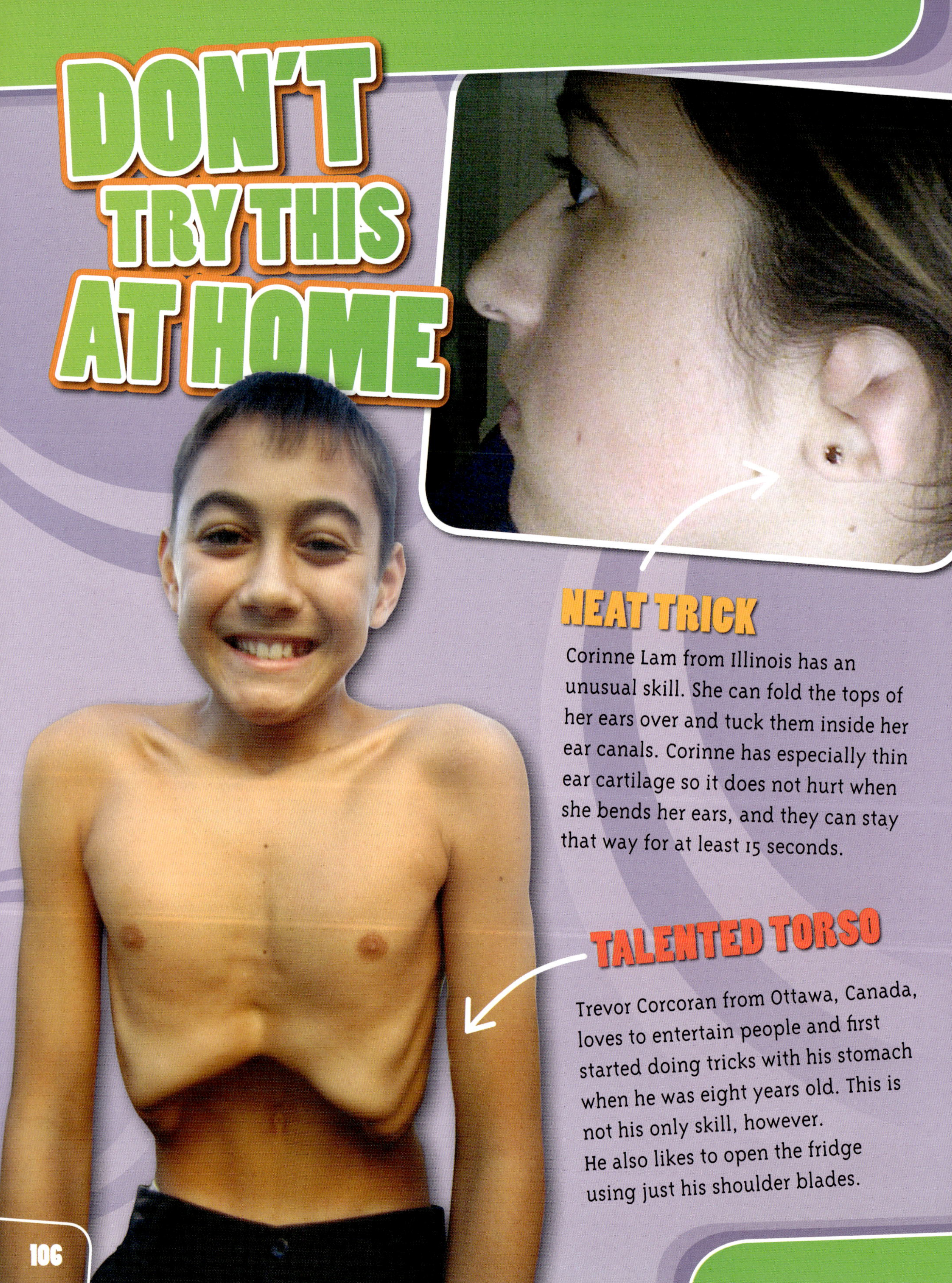

NEAT TRICK

Corinne Lam from Illinois has an unusual skill. She can fold the tops of her ears over and tuck them inside her ear canals. Corinne has especially thin ear cartilage so it does not hurt when she bends her ears, and they can stay that way for at least 15 seconds.

TALENTED TORSO

Trevor Corcoran from Ottawa, Canada, loves to entertain people and first started doing tricks with his stomach when he was eight years old. This is not his only skill, however. He also likes to open the fridge using just his shoulder blades.

Coming or Going?

Kristin Lane from San Antonio, Texas, first discovered that she could turn her foot back to front when she was six years old. The 23-year-old has joint hypermobility syndrome, which means the ligaments that connect her bones are super stretchy.

INTERVIEW

How did you discover you could bend your leg?
I found out I could turn my leg around when I was about six or seven years old. I was trying to walk like a penguin with my legs turned inward, when I realized one could go inward a little bit farther, so I decided to see how far I could turn it around. I didn't think anything of it until I did it in front of people and they would freak out.

Does it hurt when you turn them around?
There is no pain at all when I turn either one of my legs. Sometimes if I do it too much, it may feel like I overstretched it, but it's not painful. The doctor said my ligaments are like a worn-out rubber band that can stretch more than a brand-new one.

Is there anything else affected by your hypermobility syndrome?
Almost all of my joints are affected. Both legs can turn around, and I can touch my head behind my back with my hand. One of the good things about it is that I can never sprain my ankle, because if I "twist" my ankle, my ligaments can stretch and not get hurt.

WHOA, TWISTED!

BE AFRAID

Didaskaleinophobia
is the fear of going to school!
Blennophobia
is the fear of slime.
The fear of fear or of having a fear is known as
Phobophobia
Hippopotomonstrosesquippedaliophobia
is the fear of long words.
Cassandra Tainsh from England used to have a phobia of spiders until she decided to get one of her own to overcome her fear. Her pet, a giant Chilean red tarantula named Pandora, has since become her best friend, and she has even bought her a miniature TV, table and chairs, and tiny spider outfits!
WHOA!
Australian composer Arnold Schoenberg, who suffered from a fear of the number 13, was born September 13, 1874 and died on Friday, July 13, 1951.

PICTURE PERFECT

TWINS REUNITED

Bao Lulin from Guizho, China, was puzzled when strangers said hello and called her Yanfei. Eventually, she asked one of them for Yanfei's address and discovered that she had a twin sister. The girls were adopted by different families at birth, and both had no idea the other existed.

PHOTO ID

Believe it or not, this is not a photo, it is a portrait made with more than two million ink dots. Artist Miguel Endara created the image of Benjamin Kyle, a man suffering from amnesia with no ID or memory of who he is. Half the proceeds of the work will go toward helping Benjamin to find out who he is.

Singing Spaceman

Canadian astronaut Chris Hadfield attracted more than a million Twitter followers as he posted photos and videos from the International Space Station. Images from his five-month mission included pictures of life on board and views of Earth from 250 miles above the planet. As the expedition came to an end, Commander Hadfield performed his own version of David Bowie's "Space Oddity," which has been viewed more than 19 million times.

INTERVIEW

Chris, what was it like living on the International Space Station?
It was like magic—I could fly in weightlessness, and every time I looked out the window I could see a new place on the Earth. It felt like I had a superpower! Push off the wall and float across the room, do a hundred somersaults—everyday fun!

What kind of food did you eat?
Space food is mostly dried and prepackaged, or in tins/cans, so a bit boring. It has to travel a long way and be stored onboard, so it needs to last a long time. We reheat it in a little warming oven, or by injecting hot water into the packet.

By posting to Twitter, did you feel connected to Earth down below?
Being able to post to Twitter and see the thousands of replies helped keep me very connected with Earth. Social media is very—social! A nice thing to have when living in an aluminum-tube condo, high above the Earth, miles from home.

SWEET DREAMS

WHOA!

Lesley Cusack from Cheshire, England, manages to cook meals while sleepwalking!

FLYING FEATHERS

Feathers flew around the world as pillow fights were held in more than 120 cities to celebrate World Pillow Fight Day. Thousands of people took part in this massive fight in Trafalgar Square, London, England. The fights were organized by a group called Urban Playground Movement.

REAL-LIFE SLEEPING BEAUTY

Louisa Ball has missed exams, dance lessons, birthdays, and a family vacation because she was fast asleep. The British teenager suffers from a rare condition called "Sleeping Beauty Syndrome" and sleeps for weeks at a time. It began after she developed a flu-like illness.

TIE FOR THE TIRED

Sleepy office workers can nod off in comfort if they are wearing a pillow tie. The tie contains a hidden, inflatable air bag that can be blown up using a mouthpiece. It will support up to 25 pounds, which is more than twice the weight of the average human head.

CATNAP CONTEST

Spain's first siesta championship was held in a shopping mall in Madrid. Contestants had to sleep for as close to 20 minutes as possible, and extra points were awarded for original sleeping positions, the loudest snore, and the most eye-catching outfit. The overall winner received a prize of $1,330.

SKIN DEEP

BODY MAP

If you want to know the quickest route from the kidney to the lung, check out Sam Loman's map of the human body. Called *Underskin* after the London Underground in England, the Dutch artist's design shows bones and organs as stations and the body's systems as subway lines.

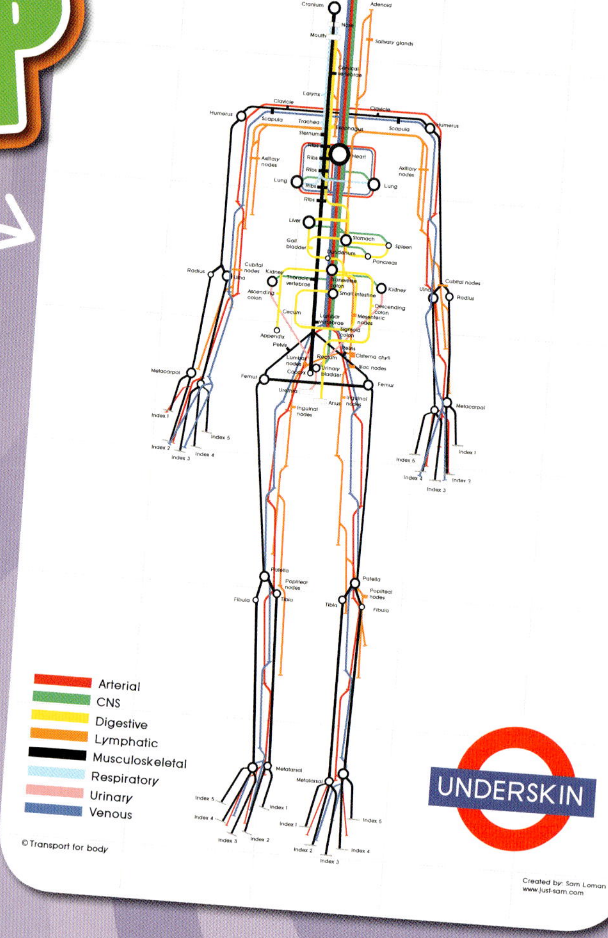

PALM PAINTINGS

Russian artist Svetlana Kolosova does not have to look far for a canvas because she paints on the palm of her left hand. Her paintings are inspired by fairy tales, but they only last for a single day before she has to wash them off.

Living Canvases

More than 29,000 bodypaint artists from 45 countries gathered in Austria in July 2013 for the 16th World Bodypainting Festival, where the themes were "Planet Food" and "Holy Geometry." Two hundred artists competed in categories, including airbrushing, special-effects bodypainting, and face painting. Huge headdresses, colored contact lenses, and jewels added the finishing touches.

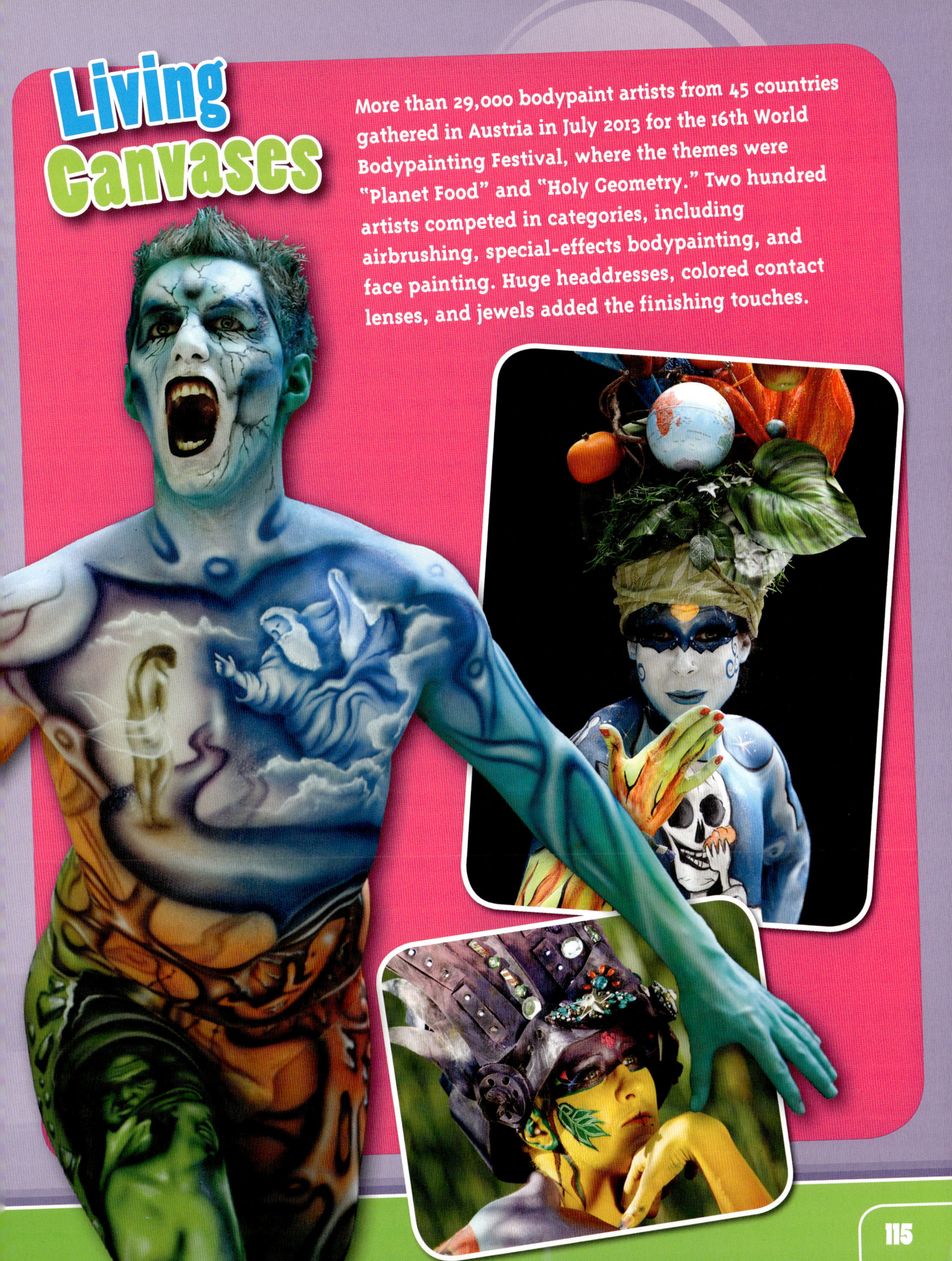

SOLE MATES

At 15 inches long, Brahim Takioullah's feet are four times the length of 19-year-old Jyoti Amge's, which measure just 3.72 inches. The 31-year-old Moroccan stands eight feet one inch tall, while two-foot-tall Jyoti, from India, is just nine inches bigger than Brahim's feet.

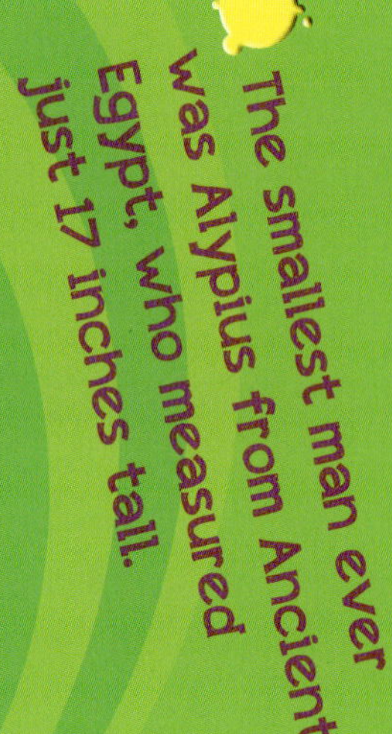

Francisco Domingo Joaquim, from Angola, can fit a Coca-Cola can inside his mouth, which can stretch to about seven inches wide.

Moustafa Ismail, 24, from Franklin, Massachusetts, has biceps that are 31 inches around!

TWO DOZEN DIGITS

Twelve-year-old Ouyang Guangchun, from China's Hunan Province, has six fingers on each hand and six toes on each foot. The family's pig gave birth to a piglet with eight legs, two mouths, and four ears just before he was born, and his mother thinks this was a sign.

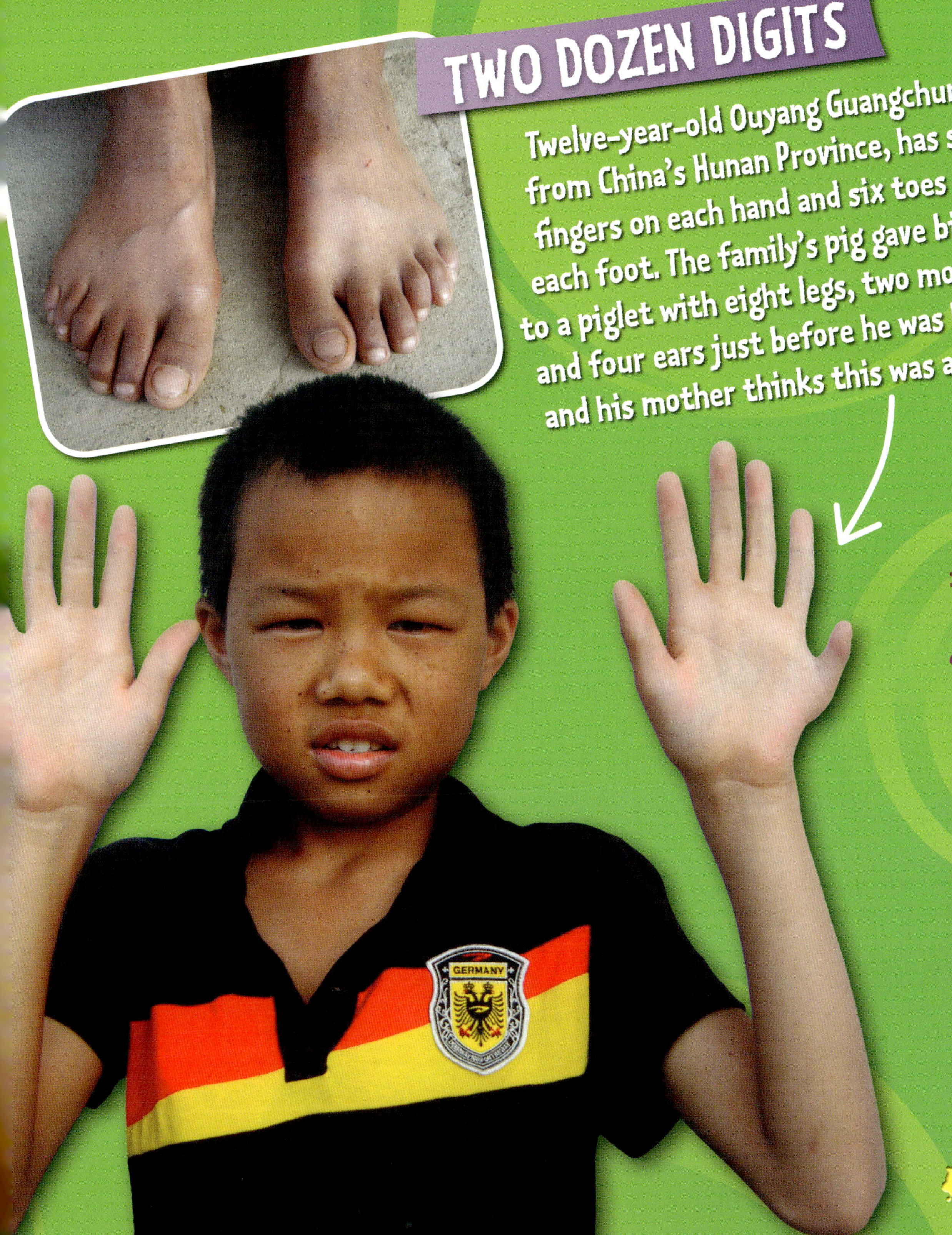

In February 2012, Wang Yujuan from Henan, China, gave birth to a massive 15-pound baby.

6
LARGER THAN LIFE

THAT'S BIG

EXOTIC PARADISE

Visitors to the Tropical Islands Resort do not need to worry about tropical storms as they swim in the lagoon and relax on the beach, surrounded by exotic plants. The resort is housed inside an enormous old airship hangar in Krausnick, Germany, which is tall enough to accommodate the Statue of Liberty.

EPIC GAME

More than 1,250 spongy red balls took flight during a massive dodgeball game at the University of Alberta, in Edmonton, Canada. A total of 4,979 students and staff members took part in the chaotic, hour-long contest at the university's Butterdome.

WHOA!

Chocolatiers from California created a six-foot-high, 10-foot-wide chocolate pyramid that weighed 18,239 pounds—as much as two adult elephants!

GIANT JIGSAW

British jigsaw addict Amanda Warrington spent 17 months completing a 24,000-piece puzzle called "Life: The Great Challenge." She had to glue each piece to her living room wall because it was the only place in her home with space for the 14-foot-wide puzzle.

MASSIVE MARGHERITA

Five pizza chefs worked for 48 hours to create a pizza 130 feet wide, with an area of almost 13,300 square feet. The chefs had to cook the dough in 5,234 batches, and used 19,800 pounds of flour, 8,800 pounds of tomato sauce, and 19,800 pounds of cheese.

HANDY PHONE

British designer Sean Miles created these "Talk to the Hand" gloves to highlight the importance of recycling old cell phones. They have a speaker unit in the thumb and a microphone built into the pinkie. They can be connected to any handset using Bluetooth.

"Kuratas" is a 13-foot-tall robot that is controlled from the one-person cockpit, or by using a smartphone. The four-ton Japanese giant is fitted with futuristic weapons, including a gun that can fire 6,000 BB pellets a minute, which shoots when the pilot smiles.

JACUZZI BOAT

A boat normally keeps you dry on the water, but the Hot Tub Boat combines a pleasure cruise with a relaxing soak. The floating hot tub has a top speed of five mph, and bathers can listen to music through a waterproof stereo system as they soak and cruise.

SNEAKER SHELTER

Next time you need a tent in a hurry, you could just pull one out of your shoes. The Walking Shelter packs a two-piece tent into net pockets attached to a pair of high-top sneakers. Pull the two halves over your head, join them together, and you have an instant shelter.

COLOSSAL CRAFTS

Nikki Douthwaite created a portrait of Lewis Hamilton using only the paper dots discarded from a hole-punch.

Herb Williams creates mosaic sculptures and portraits using up to 500,000 color crayons.

On a beach in China, 900 tents were set up in the shape of a dragon.

Ukrainian artist Svetlana Ivanchenko creates mosaics using sand, shells, and other materials found on the beach. Inspired by the Black Sea where she grew up, Svetlana painstakingly sifts through the sand and pebbles before sorting them by color. She never dyes or paints the materials.

WHOA!

Jane Perkins creates 3-D artworks using objects found in the trash. She has created versions of classic paintings such as the *Mona Lisa* and *Sunflowers*.

WHAT ARE THE CHANCES?

LUCKY ESCAPE

Scampi the kitten nearly drowned after climbing into a washing machine while his owner, Frances Leate from Colchester, England, went to fetch more clothes. She started the machine and only noticed Scampi inside ten minutes later. She rushed him to a veterinary hospital where he made a full recovery.

WHOA!

Twelve-year-old Robert Hunt from Scotland found a rare gold sovereign in his change after a shopping trip. The coin dated 1901 was worth $300.

UP, UP, AND AWAY

A helium balloon released by a six-year-old English schoolboy was found more than 10,000 miles away by a girl in Australia. Students from Joshua Blackaby's elementary school launched 300 tagged balloons as part of a school project about geography and the weather.

Toy Car Cure

Olivia Johnston-Wilder from Coventry, England, was paralyzed from the waist down after falling and breaking her back in five places. The 16-year-old feared she would never walk again until she got stuck in a toy car. As she twisted her back trying to free herself, some feeling returned to her legs. Physical therapy sessions helped her get back on her feet and she has since completed two three-mile charity runs.

DIG IN!

TASTY CAKE!

Tyrone Jacques asked British cake maker Cecilia Chalmers to create this fondant spider for a scary-themed party. He has a phobia of spiders and hoped that the edible arachnid would help him to overcome it. When it arrived, he pretended to his sons that he had found it in the garage.

CAKE HOTEL

Visitors to this London hotel can easily enjoy a midnight feast because most of the furnishings are made from cake and candy. Fourteen confectioners spent almost 2,000 hours creating the edible works of art, which included vanilla sponge pillows and rugs made from meringues and marshmallows.

PIZZA PICTURES

Food artist Prudence Staite has re-created iconic artworks by Vincent van Gogh, Claude Monet, Andy Warhol, and Edvard Munch on pizzas using ham, pepperoni, olives, vegetables, and cheese. The pizza masterpieces were commissioned by a British restaurant chain to celebrate their summer menu.

PRUDENCE'S FAVORITE PIECE

"*Sunflowers* was the hardest pizza I have ever made. I had to use a tiny scalpel blade to cut the yellow peppers and pepperoni to make the sunflowers, and to cut tiny pieces from spring onions and asparagus for the leaves. I think the grated cheese looks a lot like the thick paint Van Gogh used."

SWEET SNEAKERS

Dutch designer Joost Goudriaan's convincing chocolate replicas of the Nike Air Max 1 sneakers are accurate down to the tiniest detail. They are available in milk or white chocolate and come with a contract stating that the buyer is obliged to eat them.

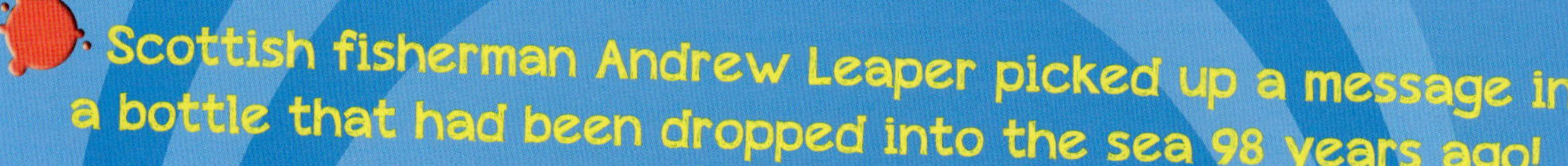

Scottish fisherman Andrew Leaper picked up a message in a bottle that had been dropped into the sea 98 years ago!

NO WAY!

CART LOUNGER

American-born designer Mike Bouchet has given this shopping cart a new life by removing the sides and transforming it into a sun lounger. The chair comes with foam pillows, and the child seat forms a headrest. Future fixtures will include armrests, side tables, and an iPod dock.

Four-year-old Dylan Hayes of Colorado survived unhurt after falling three floors and landing on his feet!

Your head ages faster than your feet!

WHAT COULD GO WRONG?

If you were trying to think of the safest way to deliver 500 eggs, balancing them on a bicycle might not be your first choice. This man was photographed holding onto a towering stack of egg cartons with one hand as he rode through the busy streets of Marrakech, Morocco.

Rubber is one of the ingredients in bubblegum.

WHOA!

Each year, David Schuler of Madison, Missouri, drives a 2,600-mile round-trip to stock up on pizzas from his favorite pizza restaurant in Stoughton, Massachusetts!

FOOD FOR THOUGHT

DELICIOUS DRESS

Donna Millington-Day's bridal-gown cake stands six feet tall and would serve 2,400 people. It took the cake maker from Birmingham, England, a week to make the edible dress, which is decorated with more than 50 pounds of icing and hundreds of pearls.

SURREAL CEREALISM

Where most people see breakfast, Ernie Button sees art. The photographer from Phoenix, Arizona, spends up to a week constructing scenes that combine breakfast cereal with natural backdrops. His works include schools of fish, pyramids in the desert, and rural landscapes.

CREEPY CONFECTIONERY

Even a dedicated chocoholic might think twice before tasting one of the realistic creepy-crawlies created by English confectioners Chris Verraes and Sarah Hardy. In addition to this chocolate worm, their candy creations include a snail with a creamy green filling and a toad with popping candy warts.

STICKY PORTRAITS

Anna-Sofiya Matveeva creates portraits from used chewing gum. She needs up to 1,000 pieces for each picture, so the Ukrainian artist asks friends and family to help with the chewing, because it is an enzyme in saliva that makes the gum workable. Each portrait contains saliva from at least 12 people.

ANNA USING THE GUM

CHEWED-UP GUM

BRIGHT IDEAS

The XploreAir X1 flying bicycle is supported by a parachute and propelled by a huge fan, which is powered by a biofuel motor. It can reach a height of 4,000 feet and fly at 25 mph for up to three hours. The bike even includes a built-in tent.

Izhar Gafni has invented a cardboard bike that can support a rider nearly 20 times its weight. The Israeli engineer learned how to fold cardboard into strong shapes by studying structures such as honeycomb and birds' nests. Varnish protects it from getting wet and old car tires are used on the wheels.

Although modern canned food dates back to 1810, the can opener was not invented until 1870.

WHOA!

Frank Epperson invented the Popsicle in 1905 when he was 11 years old. He discovered it when he left a drink outside overnight with the stir stick in it, and the drink froze.

Play-Doh was originally invented as wallpaper cleaner.

Slinky toys were invented by naval mechanic Richard James, who realized another possible use of the springs he was making for ships.

SUPERMARKET SHOP

MEAT LOAF

Long lines form outside the Domalaon Bakery in Manila during the Christmas holiday season as customers wait to buy their special pig-shaped loaves. Suckling pig, which symbolizes thrift and prosperity, is a traditional part of the Christmas and New Year celebrations in the Philippines, so the bread makes a perfect centerpiece.

COMFORT FOOD

Kate Jenkins's crocheted food is a feast for the eyes. The British artist re-creates well-known foods in wool with a witty twist, such as this Crochet Cola can of Coca-Cola. Her other creations include ketchup—labeled Katez Tomato Stitchup; french fries with tiny faces and berets; and a burrito wearing a sombrero and a mustache.

Dinner with Shimmer

Food from the Deli Garage looks as if it belongs in a mechanic's workshop. Flavored oils are packaged in oilcans, while a tub of chocolate spread looks like filler and comes with a plastic spreader. Now the German company is selling a product that adds sparkle to a boring meal. Food Finish edible paint comes in spray cans and is available in metallic silver, gold, red, and blue.

SIZE MATTERS

TRICK OF THE EYE

Things are not always as they appear in Japan's Takao Trick Art Museum. The woman on the left looks smaller than the one on the right because the room is distorted. The walls, ceiling, and floor are slanted, and the right corner is much closer to the observer than the left.

OUTSIZED ALICE

Spanish artist Cristina Lucas created this art installation, called *Alice*, in a courtyard building in the ancient Spanish town of Córdoba. She was inspired by Alice from *Alice's Adventures in Wonderland*, who grew into a giant after eating a piece of cake with "Eat Me" written on it.

BIG BALL

This massive inflatable red ball was displayed at sites around Paris, France, as part of Kurt Perschke's RedBall Project. The American artist is taking the ball on a tour of the world's cities to encourage people to use their imagination, inspired by the playful nature of the ball.

WHOA!

A 70-foot-high sand sculpture was created by 30 artists over 70 days in Zhoushan, China. The piece depicted a Nigerian story of how a hummingbird became the king of all animals.

GIANT RUBBER DUCKY

Thousands of Hong Kong residents turned out to say good-bye to a 54-foot-tall rubber duck, which had been on display in the harbor for just over a month, as it left for the next stop on its 'round-the-world tour. Dutch artist Florentijn Hofman created the duck, named *Spreading Joy Around the World*.

PHOTO CREDITS

Ripley Entertainment Inc. and the editors of this book wish to thank the following photographers, agents, and other individuals for permission to use and reprint the following photographs in this book. Any photographs included in this book that are not acknowledged below are property of the Ripley Archives. Great effort has been made to obtain permission from the owners of all material included in this book. Any errors that may have been made are unintentional and will gladly be corrected in future printings if notice is sent to Ripley Entertainment Inc., 7576 Kingspointe Parkway, Suite 188, Orlando, Florida 32819.

COVER: Erik "The Lizardman" Sprague — © Allen Falkner

BACK COVER: clockwise — Parrot in sweater — Rebecca Blagg; Iron Girl running — Paul Ark; Goat riding horse — Newfoundland & Labrador Tourism

CONTENTS PAGES: 2: Spider-Man beard—Stephen Brown of PhotosbyDash; Iron Girl—Karen Thibodeaux; **3:** Church that looks like a chicken—John Wincoff Photography; Professor Splash— Rob Griffith/AP/Press Association Images; Parrot in knitted jumper— Rebecca Blagg

INTRO PAGES: 7: Fabric chef—Jeannie J Martin, artist and designer of unique, realistic, fabric food sculptures; Breathing-in stomach—Nancy, Rick, and Trevor Corcoran; Goat riding a horse—Newfoundland & Labrador Tourism

CHAPTER 1: 10: Yoga on a mountaintop—Lukasz Warzecha/ Caters News; Cliff diver—Eric Mohl/Caters News; **11:** Highline musicians—Alexandre Buisse/Caters News; **12:** Excavator on top of building—Rex/Quirky China News; Painting Eiffel Tower—© Bertrand Rieger/Hemis/Corbis; **13:** Counting coins—Europics; Man who raised crocodile—Rex/Cameron L'Estrange/Newspix; **14:** Kamikazi man—Rex/Mike Keating/ Newspix; Snow skier—Rex/Scott Markewitz/Solent News; **15:** Iron Girl running—Paul Ark; Iron Girl cycling—Karen Thibodeaux; Iron Girl standing—John Conroy; Interview icon—PremiumVector – Shutterstock.com; **16–17:** Nik Wallenda crossing Grand Canyon—Tiffany Brown/AP Press Association Images; **17:** Circles—Redshinestudio – Shutterstock.com; **18:** Man fought off python—Paul Tarantino; Head in lion's mouth—Reuters/Gleb Garanich; **19:** Climbing rock—Rex/Sam Bie/ PETZL/Solent News; **20:** Man pulls airplane with ear—Rex/HAP/Quirky China News; **22:** Cornflake feat—Rex/Mick Hobday/Solent News; Tuk tuk journey—Rex/www.tuktuktravels.com; **23:** Extreme ironing—Kevin Krupitzer/Caters News; Family travel around the world—Gallo Images/Rex Features; **24:** World's tallest water slide—Caters News Agency Ltd; Tall carousel—Rex/IBL; **25:** Professor Splash—Rob Griffith/AP/Press Association Images; **26–27:** Stunt planes—Rex/Alex Coppel/Newspix; **27:** Circles—Redshinestudio – Shutterstock.com; **28:** BASE jumping—AFP/Getty Images; Mountain walkway—Rex/HAP/ Quirky China News; **29:** London Eye stunt—Dangerman: The Incredible Mr Goodwin airs on Watch (Sky 109/Virgin 124/ BT 857) (c)UKTV/Watch; Interview icon—PremiumVector – Shutterstock.com

CHAPTER 2: 32: Monkey with apples in mouth—Olga Dmitrieva/SellYourPhoto.net; Spider on a spider—Caters News Agency Ltd; **33:** Cross-eyed cat—Rex/Mary Buchanan; Zebra with spots—Rex/Paul Goldstein; **34:** Parrot in sweeter—Rebecca Blagg; Pig in the city—Rex/Glenn Barnes/Newspix; **35:** Tiger living with man—Rex/Gallo Images; **36–37:** Birds shaped like a giant bird—Rex/Robert Wolstenholme/Solent News; **37:** Circles—Redshinestudio – Shutterstock.com; **38:** Pelican caught in whale's mouth—Rob Bishop/ SellYourPhoto.net; Dolphin playing basketball—Sergio Longhi/SellYourPhoto.net; **39:** Bird nesting on traffic signals—Caters News Agency Ltd; Diving pigs—Reuters/ Stringer; **40:** Woman living with cats—Caters News Agency Ltd; Walking the sheep—AFP/Getty Images; **41:** Charlie Parker with snake—Rex/Craig Borrow/Newspix; Charlie Parker with frogs—Rex/David Caird/Newspix; **42:** Woofstock—Rex/ KeystoneUSA-Zuma; **43:** Goat riding horse—Newfoundland & Labrador Tourism; **44:** Dog sits on buffalo—Reuters/Mohsin Raza; Chipmunk eating peanut—Rex/Richard Bishop/ Solent News; **45:** Tiny ponies in house—Caters News Agency Ltd; Owls living under mop—Rex/Richard Austin; **46–47:** Close-up bug—Donald Jusa/Solent News/ Rex; **47:** Circles—Redshinestudio – Shutterstock.com; **48:** Albino hedgehog—East News Press Agency; Dog feeding lamb—Rex/Richard Austin; **49:** Man kissing cheetah—Lilia Tkachenko/SellYourPhoto.net; Hugging elephants—Rex/Guus Quaedvlieg/Solent News; **50:** Donkey saved sheep—Rex/Dobson Agency; **50–51:** Hippo saving wildebeest—Caters News Agency Ltd; **51:** Squirrel saving baby—Rex/Carla Brandon/Solent News

CHAPTER 3: 54: Spotted lake—Caters News Agency Ltd; Red mountain—Rex/Harry Lichtman/Solent News; **55:** Ice pancakes—Caters News Agency Ltd; Red lake—Rex/Newspix; **56:** Prison hotel—Rex/Hotel Het Arresthuis; Tent van—Rex/Firebox.com; **57:** Egg carton spitfire—Rex; Man carries house—© Photoshot; **58:** Scary tree—Getty Images; Lumberjacks—Courtesy Humboldt State University Library; **59:** Artist carves drawings from mushrooms—Rex/Corey Corcoran/Solent News; **60:** Fastest buggy—Rex/Geoffrey Robinson; **61:** Decorated potholes—Rex/Tim Stewart News; **62:** Garbage hotel—Rex/Ray Tang; Chocolate room—photograph by Ria Novosti, Camera Press London; **63:** Salt hotel—Rex/Pedro Rocha/Solent News; Wendy houses—Barcroft Media via Getty Images; **64:** Circles—Redshinestudio – Shutterstock.com; **64–65:** Flies—xpixel – Shutterstock. com; Malawi Lake—Roland Eric Stanley Ellis; **66:** Giant tree house—Caters News Agency Ltd; **67:** Chicken church—John Wincoff Photography; Man who built his own castle—Caters News Agency Ltd; **68:** Snow roll on windsrceen—SWNS; Sandstorm in China—Rex/HAP/Quirky China News; **69:** UFO cloud—Caters News Agency Ltd; Upside-down rainbow—Rex/ Alex Parkinson/Solent News; **70:** Panda hotel—Reuters/China Daily; **71:** Van turned into swimming pool—Caters News Agency Ltd; **72:** House made of wood—Rex/Mark Edward Smith/Solent News; YouTube shower curtain—Rex/Meninos; **73:** Astronaut duvet—Rex/Tim Stet/Snurk, LED fabric—Rex

CHAPTER 4: 76: IKEA wedding—Rex/James D. Morgan; Makepeace island—Rex/James D. Morgan; **77:** Hug for a Coca-Cola—Rex/Coca-Cola Singapore/Solent News; Re-create wedding pictures after 88 years—Rex/HAP/Quirky China News; **78:** Carl Warner foodscape—Barcroft Media via Getty Images; Flying sushi trays—Reuters/Neil Hall; **79:** Fabric chef—Jeannie J Martin, artist and designer of unique, realistic, fabric food sculptures; Interview icon—PremiumVector – Shutterstock.com; **80–81:** Art using light—Darren Pearson/Caters News; **81:** Circles—Redshinestudio – Shutterstock.com; **82:** Tiny helicopter—Reuters/Yuya Shino; Tiny scissors—Dmitry Okhotsky/Caters News; **83:** Tiny clockwork motorcycle—Caters News Agency Ltd; Tiny houses—Rex/Natwerk; **84–85:** Light-up bike—Rex/Solent News; **85:** Circles—Redshinestudio – Shutterstock.com; **86:** Dress that paints itself—Rex/Anouk Wipprecht/Solent News; Human tail—Rex/Geoffrey Robinson; **87:** Car boat—Wenn; Kob Levi shoes—Rex/Kobi Levi/Solent News; **88:** Solving Rubik's Cube blind—Sameer Doshi/Caters News; Man plays piano to blind elephants—Caters News Agency Ltd; **89:** Blind man does extreme sports—Caters News Agency Ltd; **90:** Lady who gave budgie CPR—Rex/ Mark Brake/Newspix; Sleeping with snakes—Reuters/Erik De Castro; **91:** Birds who believe a cuddly toy is their mom—Rex/ Bournemouth News; Penguin with heart marking—Sue Flood/ Caters News; **92:** House illusion—Rex/Julian Makey; **93:** *Bridezillas*—NY Daily News via Getty Images; **94:** *Lord of the Rings* tattoo—Paul McCracken; Homer Simpson's car—David Moore/Caters News; **95:** Top image of matchstick Hogwarts School— Rex Features

CHAPTER 5: 98: Man lifts bricks with teeth—Rex/Zuma; Contortionist in a tin—Reuters/Kim Kyung-Hoon; **99:** Very long hair—Rex/HAP/Quirky China News; **100:** Lizard cure—© Ashley Gilbertson/VII /Corbis; Sand cure—Reuters/ Nasser Nuri; **101:** Fish cure—Rex/KeystoneUSA-Zuma; Mud bath cure—Reuters/Daniel Becerril; **102:** Spider-Man beard—Stephen Brown of PhotosbyDash; **104:** Throwing water ritual—AFP/Getty Images; **104–105:** Strong man—Reuters/ Jessica Rinaldi; **105:** Man in ice box for 64 hours—Ariel Schalit/AP/Press Association Images; **106:** Girl bends ears over—Corinne Lam; Breathing-in stomach—Nancy, Rick, and Trevor Corcoran; **107:** Girl bends feet backward—Kristin Lane; Interview icon—PremiumVector – Shutterstock.com; **108–109:** Girl who conquered fear of spiders—rossparry.co.uk/ syndication; **109:** Circles—Redshinestudio – Shutterstock.com; **110:** Discovered twins— Rex/HAP/Quirky China News; Lifelike portrait of man—Miguel Endara/Rex; **111:** Chris Hadfield view from space—Chris Hadfield © Canadian Space Agency, 2013; Interview icon—PremiumVector – Shutterstock.com; **112:** Pillow fight—Reuters/Luke MacGrego; Louisa Ball sleeping—worldwidefeatures.com; **113:** Pillow desk—Rex/ Solent News; Sleeping contest—Paul White/AP/Press Association Images; **114:** London Underground body map—Sam Loman-www.just-sam.com; Palm art—Svetlana Kolosova/ Rex Features; **115:** Bodypainting festival—Reuters/Heinz-Peter Bader; **116:** Largest and smallest feet—Rex; **117:** Extra digits on feet and hands—Rex/Quirky China News

CHAPTER 6: 120: Large indoor beach—Tropical Islands; Giant game of dodgeball—Jason Franson/The Canadian Press/Press Association Images; **121:** Jigsaw puzzle wall—Caters News Agency Ltd; Giant pizza—Rex/Solent News;**122:** Glove phone—O2/Rex Features; Giant robot—Reuters/Kim Kyung-Hoon; **123:** Hot tub boat—Rex/Cameron Zegers/Solent News; Tent shoes—Solent News/Rex Features; **124–125:** Sand art—Svetlana Ivanchenko/SellYourPhoto.Net; **125:** Circles—Redshinestudio – Shutterstock.com; **126:** Kitten in washing machine—Rex/ Eastnews; Balloon journey—Dan James/Caters News; **127:** Girl walks again—Caters News Agency; **128:** Sugar spider—Bournemouth News/Rex Features; Edible cake hotel—Rex/Geoff Pugh; **129:** Pizza art portraits—Shaun Walker, www. sawphotography.co.uk; Chocolate shoe—Rex/Solent News; **130:** Sun lounger shopping trolley—Rex/Mike Bouchet; **131:** Egg cartons on bike—© Pascal Deloche/Godong/ Corbis; **132:** Wedding dress cake—Life-sized wedding dress cake designed and made by Donna Millington-Day & daughter Hannah, of Fairytale Cake Company UK for The National Wedding Show 2013 which now stands proud their Birmingham Branch shop window; Cereal art—Ernie Button/Caters News; **133:** Chocolate bugs—Rex/Chris Verraes; Chewing gum art—Reuters/Gleb Garanich; **134:** Flying to work—Rex/Jonathan Hordle; **135:** Cardboard bike—Iarael-CardBoardBike/Reuters/Baz Ratner; Circles—Redshinestudio – Shutterstock.com; **136:** Bread shaped like a pig—Reuters/ Cheryl Ravelo; Crochet Coca-Cola—Rex/Bournemouth News; **137:** Edible food spray—Ulrike Kirmse; **138:** 3-D room—EPA/ Christopher Jue; *Alice in Wonderland* art—Reuters/Marcelo del Pozo; **139:** Giant ball—Reuters/Charles Platiau; Giant duck—Rex/Imaginechina